DEEP DEEP SPACE

&

SCI FI

COLORING BOOK

2 BOOK BUNDLE

DEEP DEEP SPACE

Outer Space Coloring Book

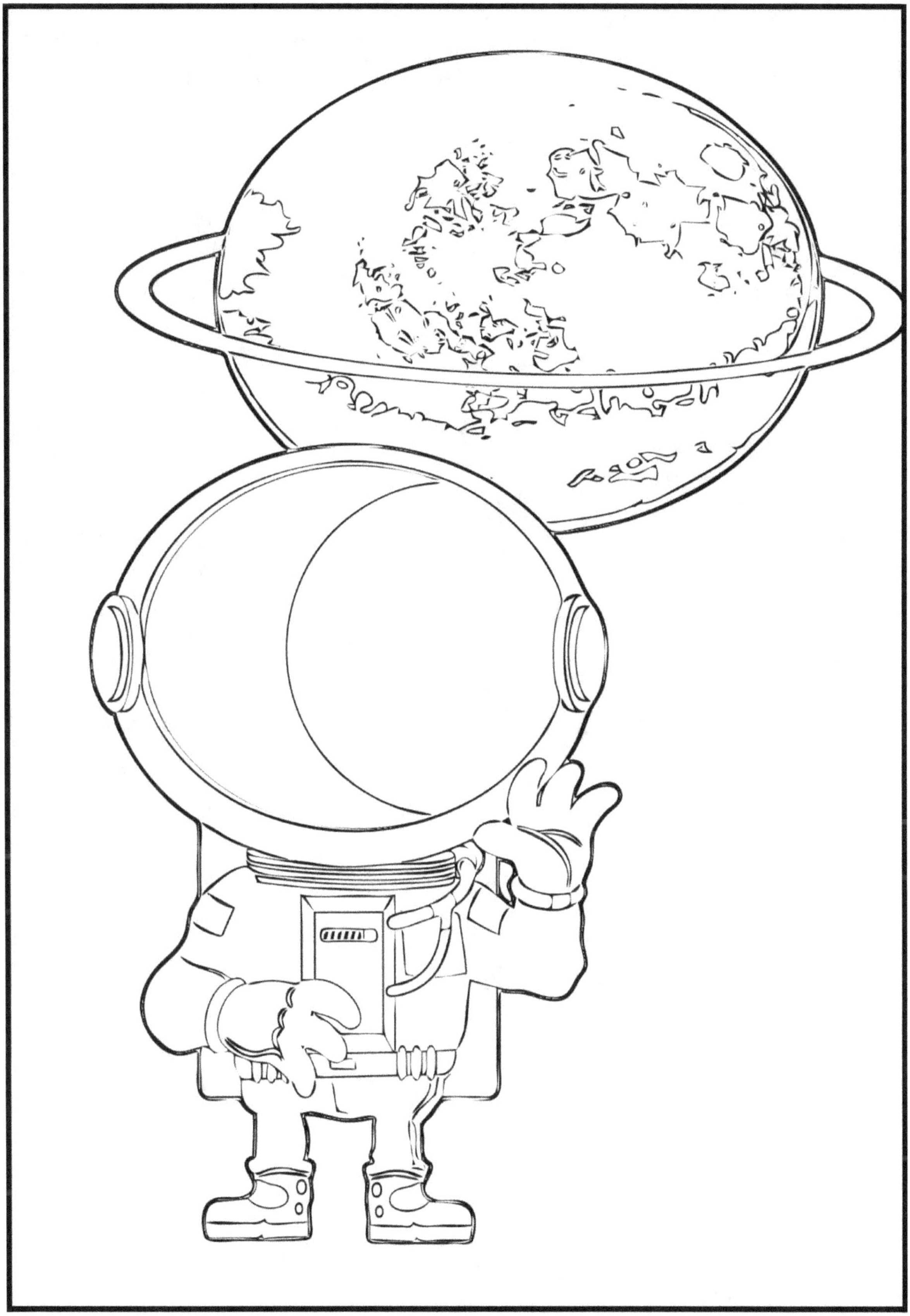

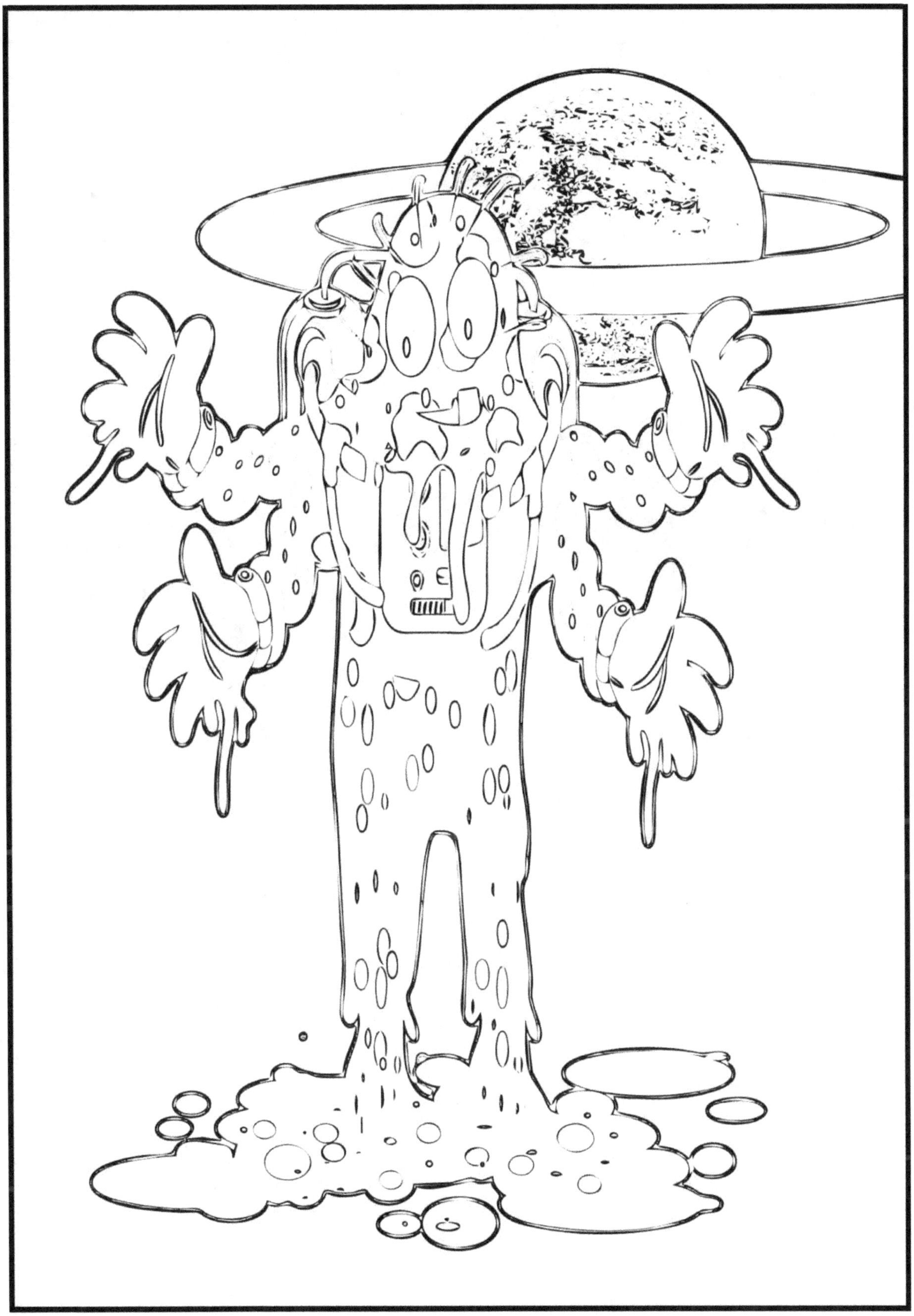

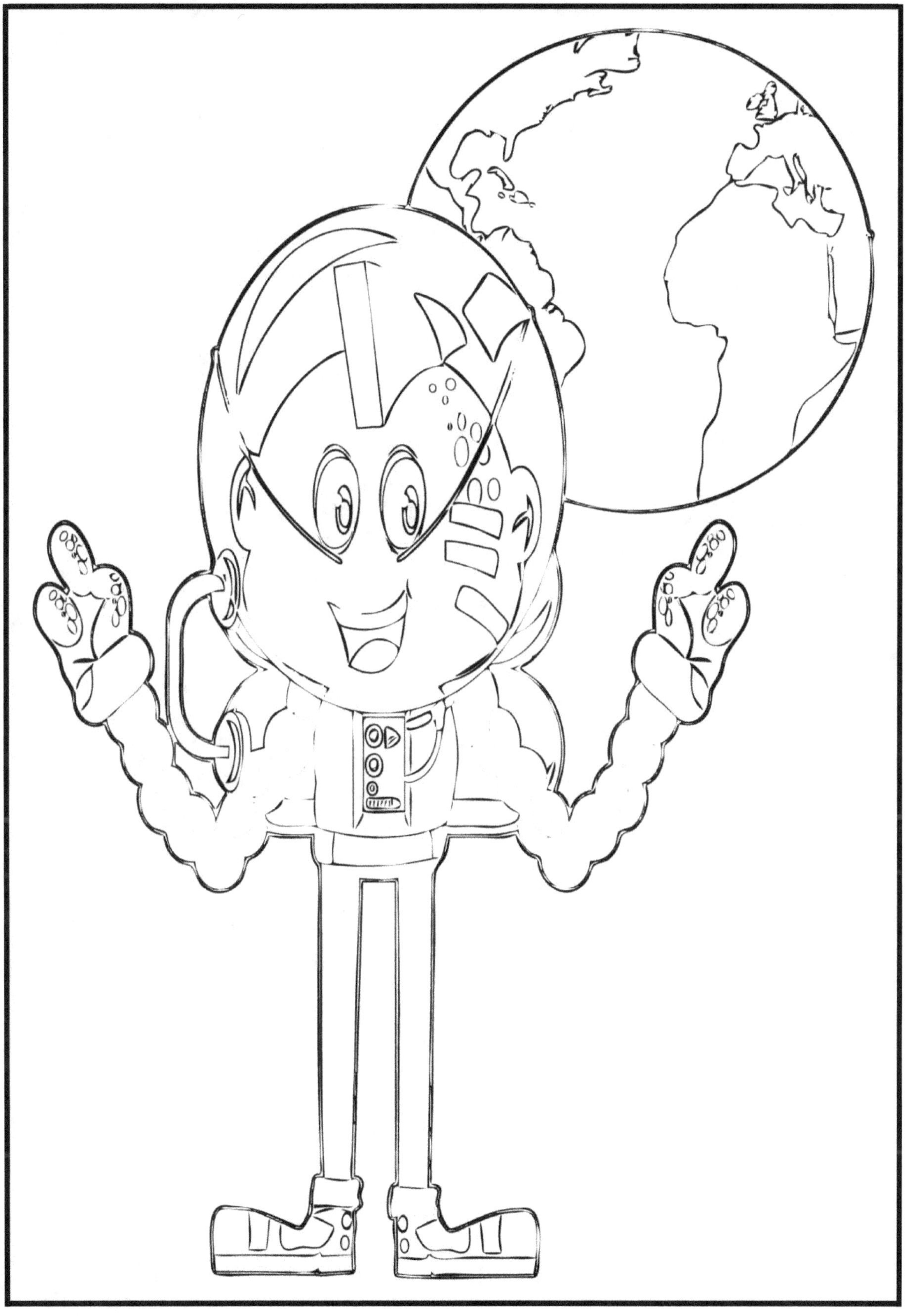

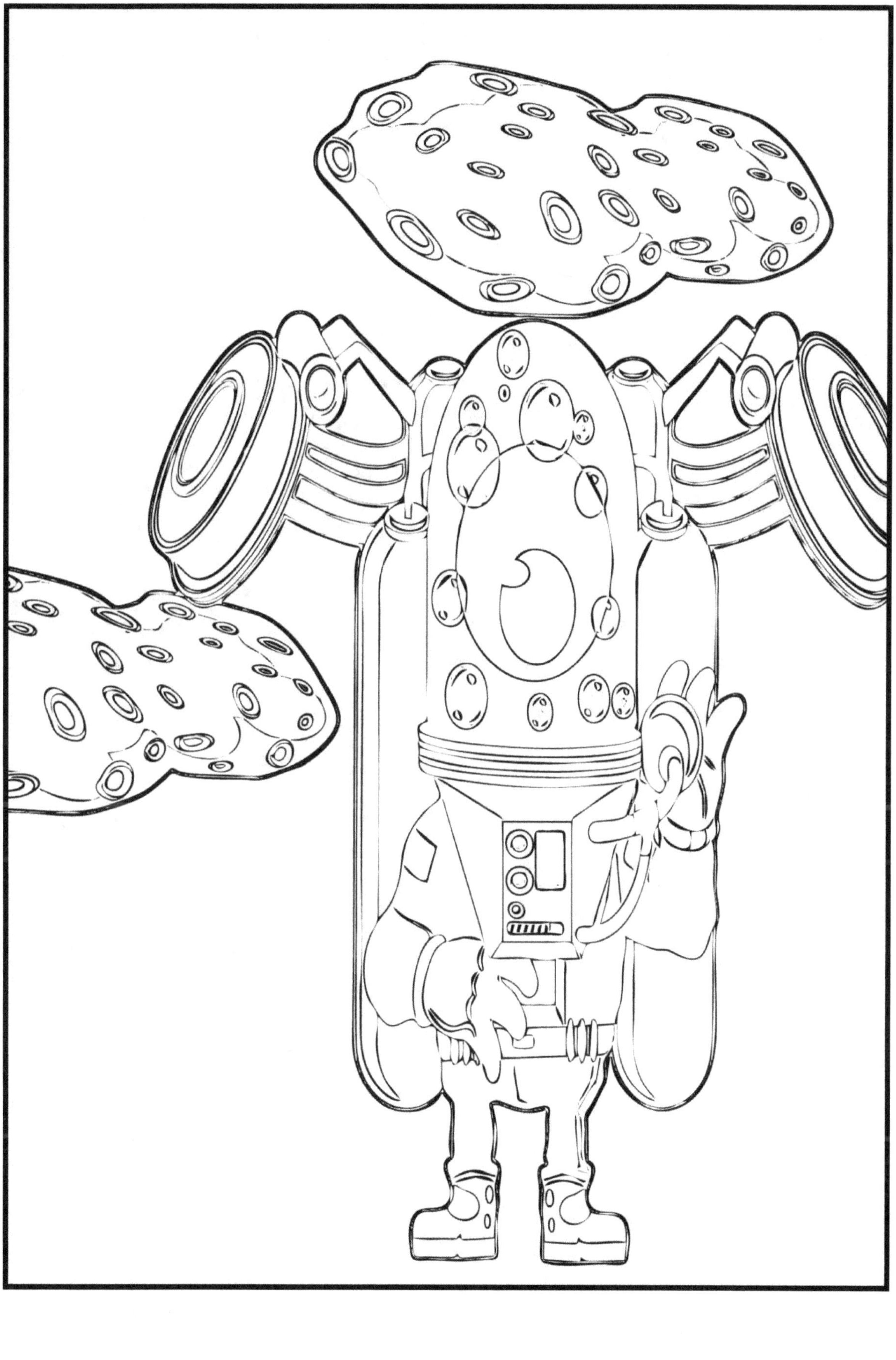

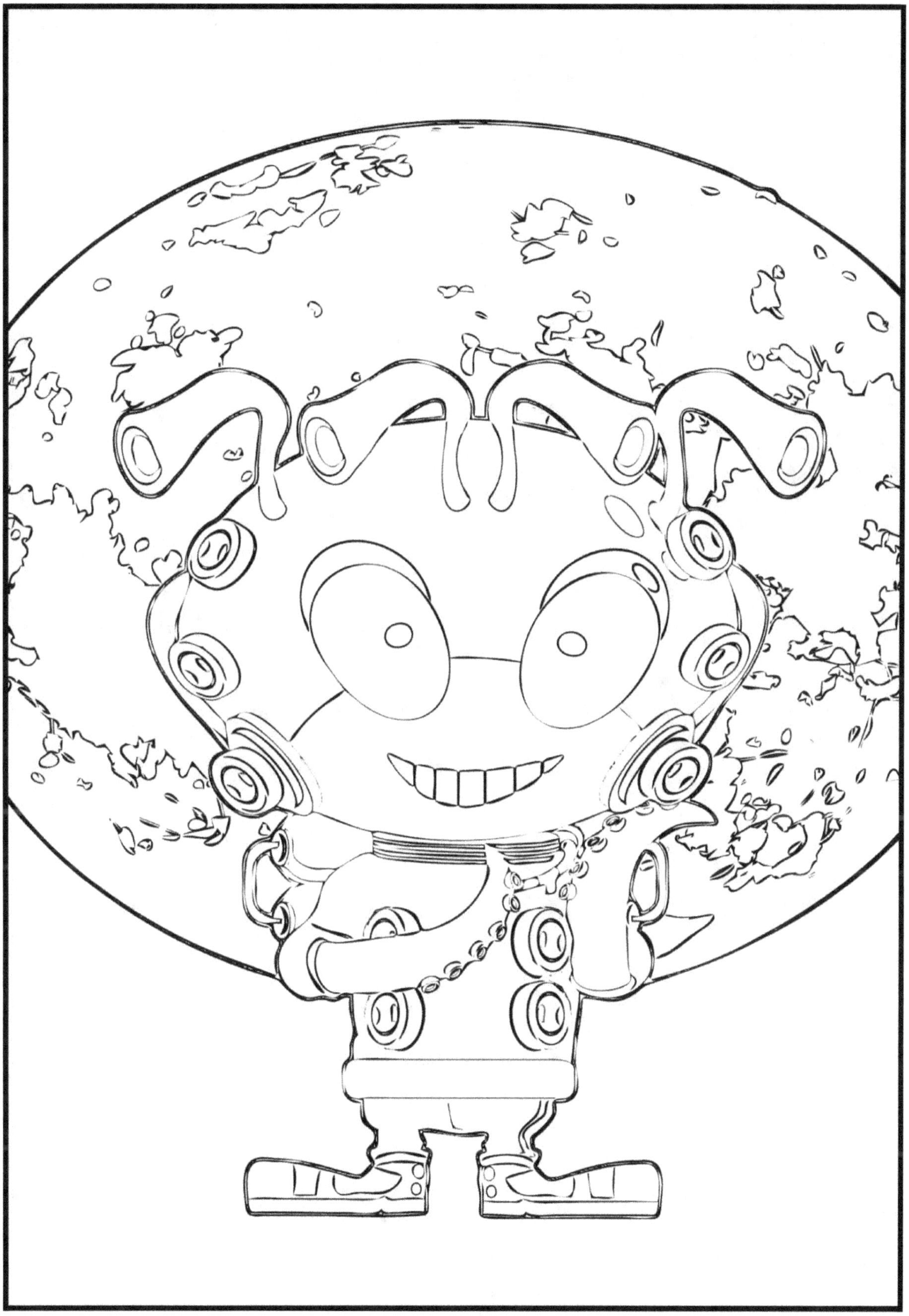

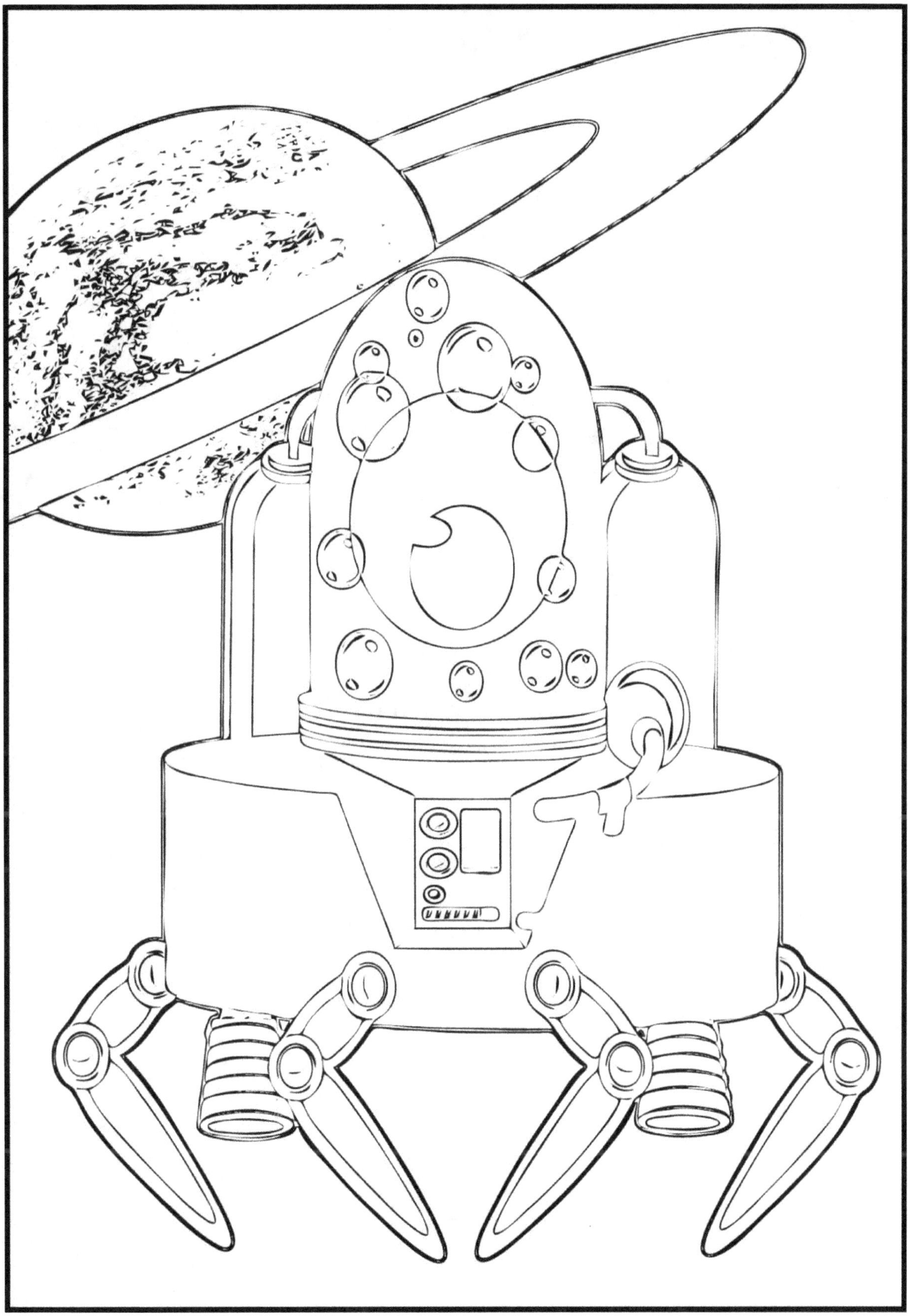

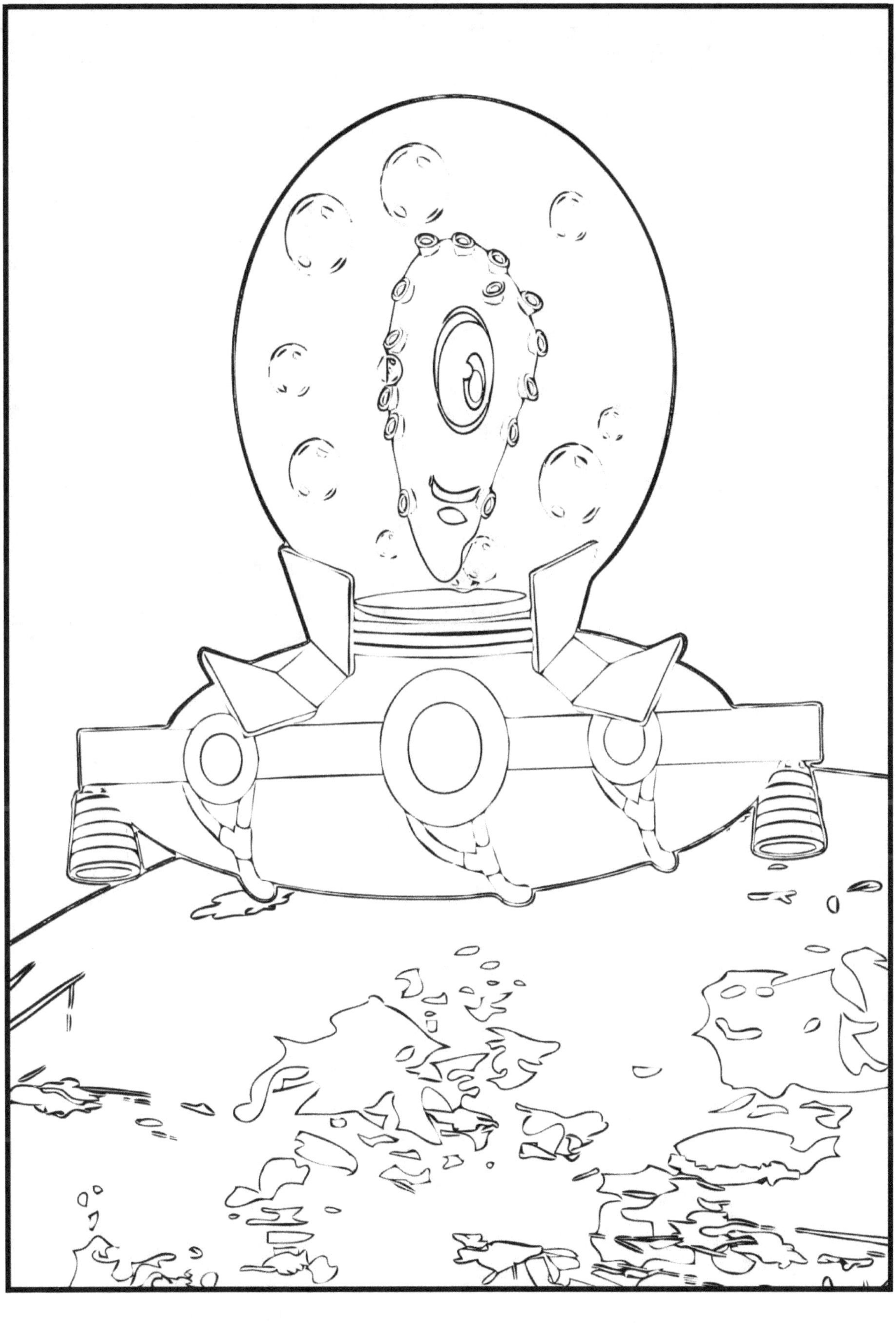

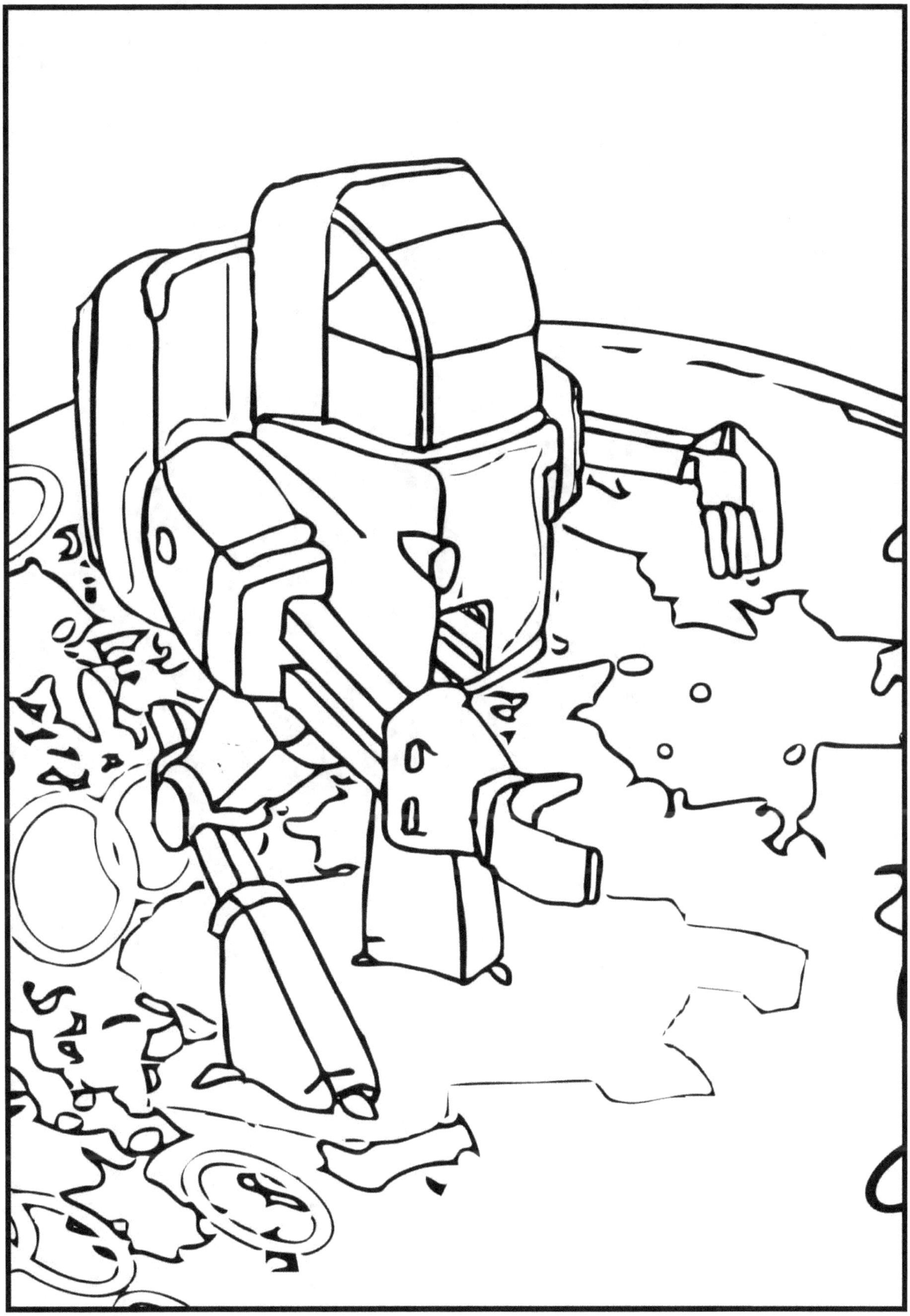

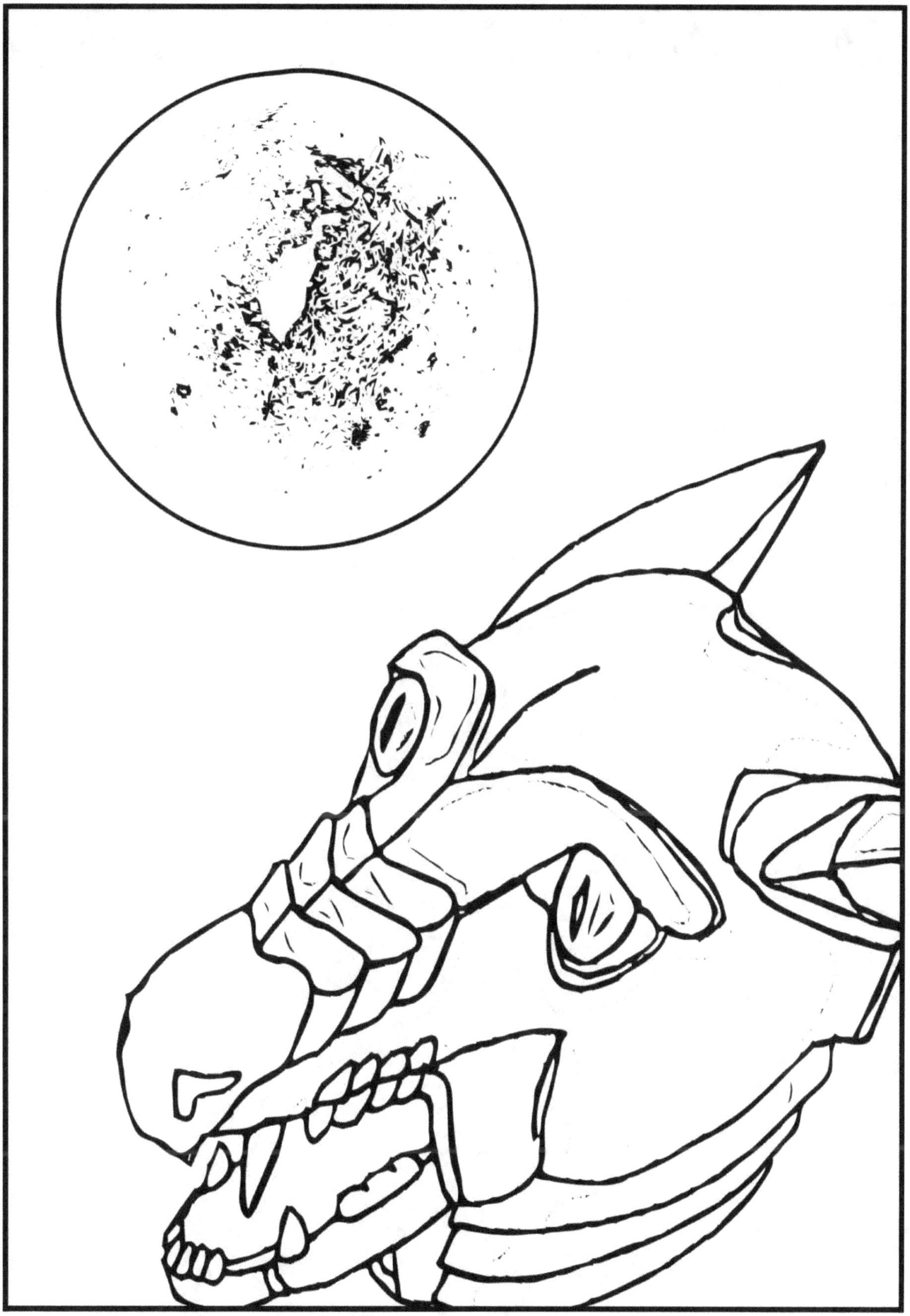

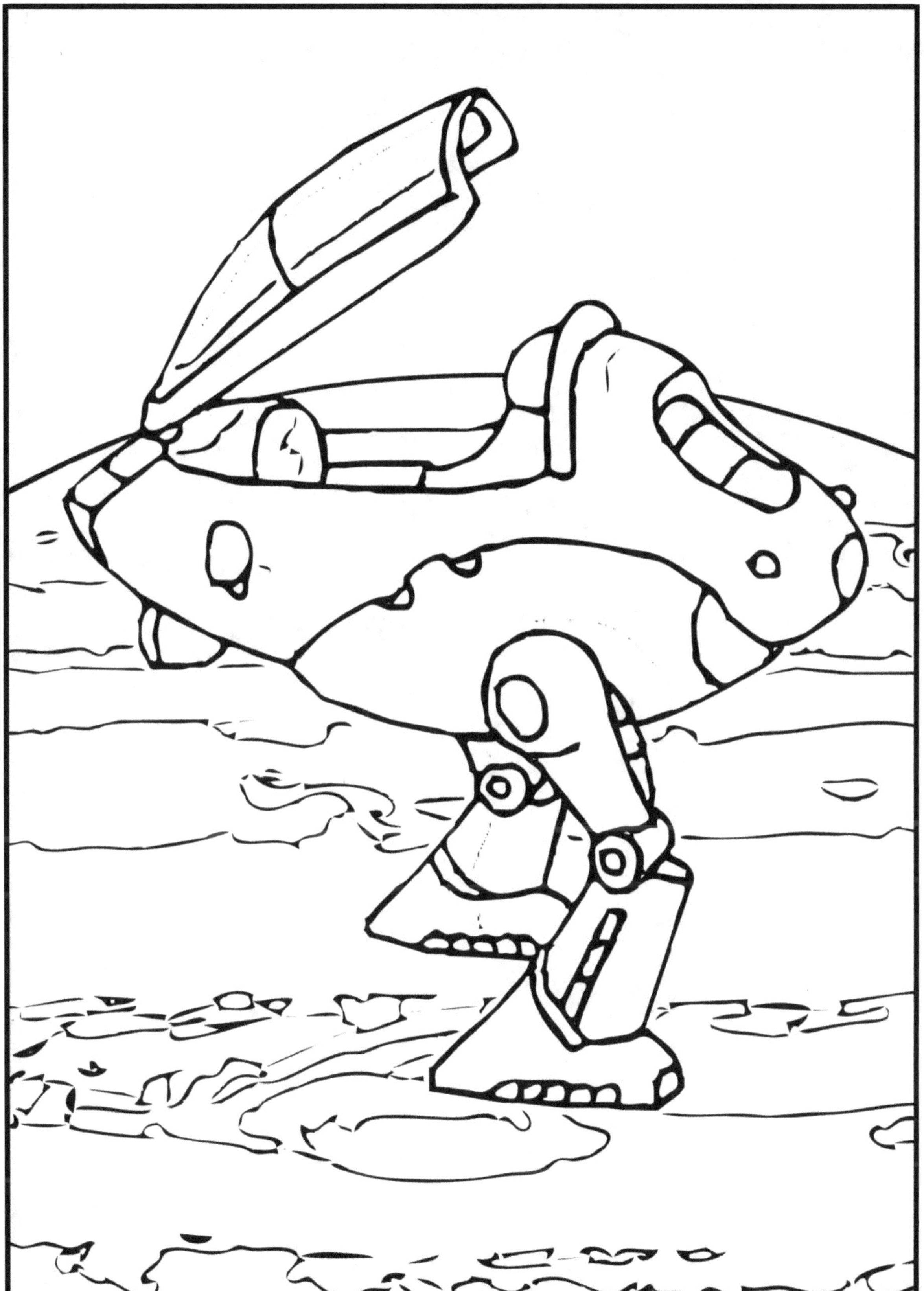

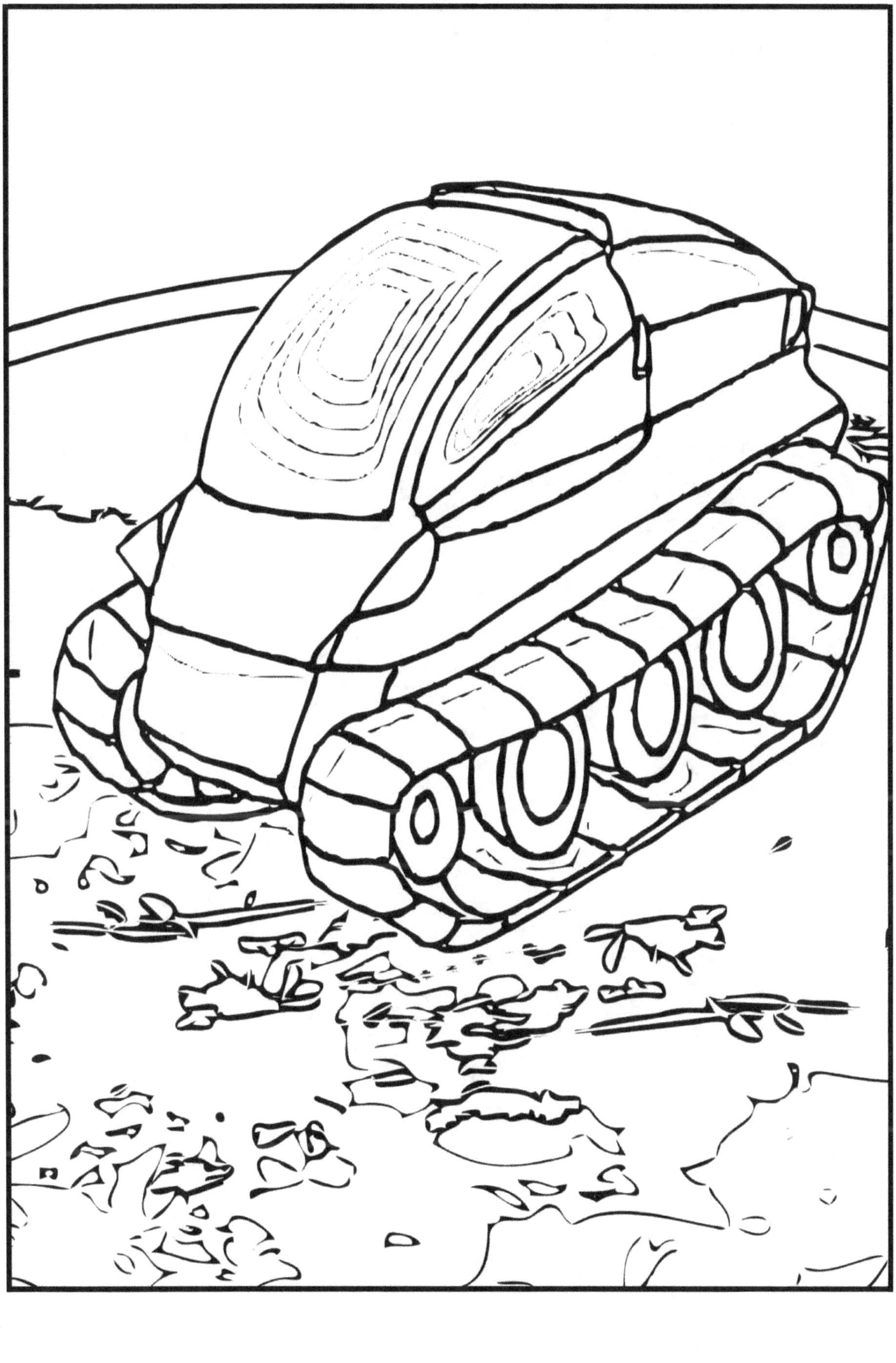

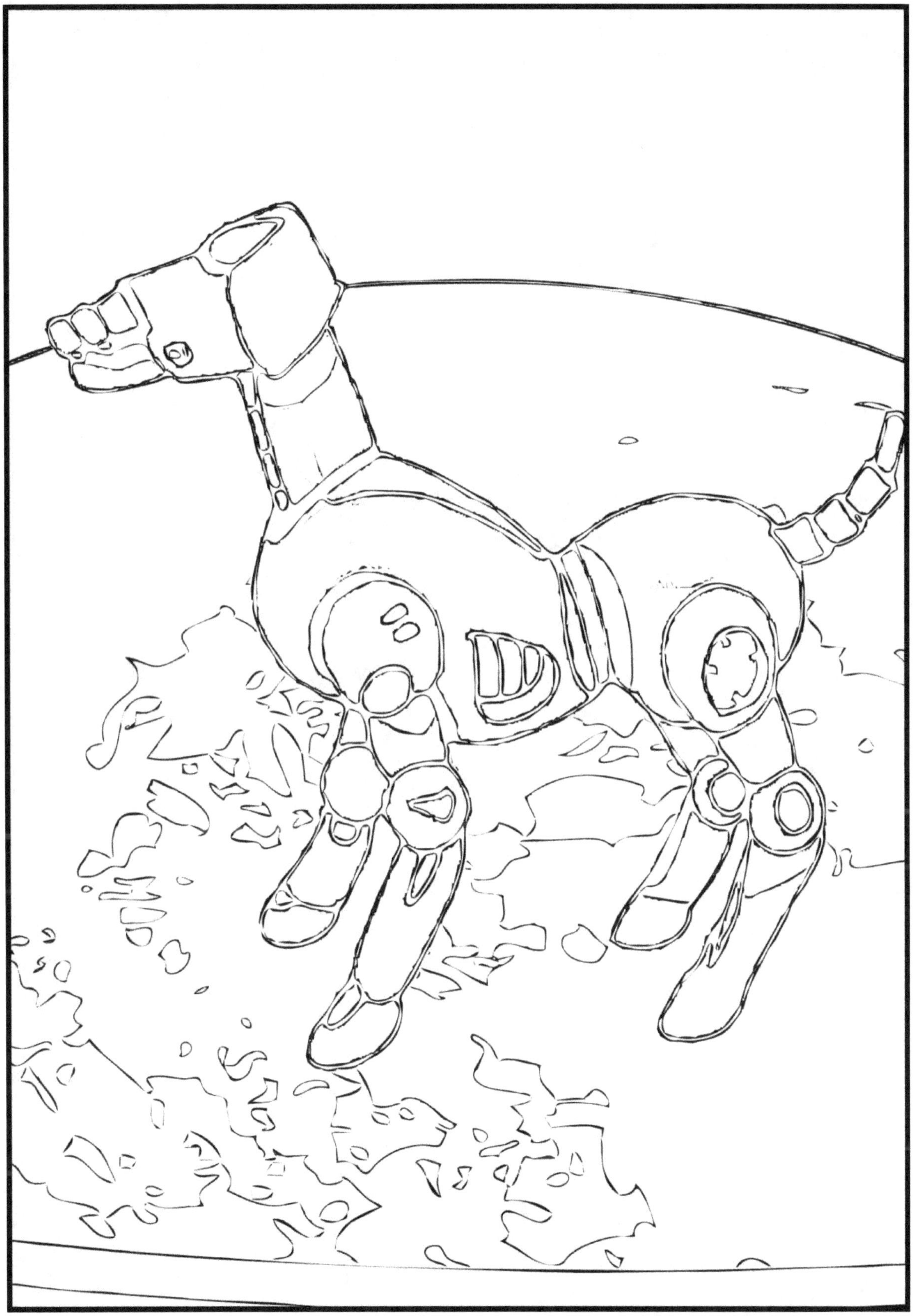

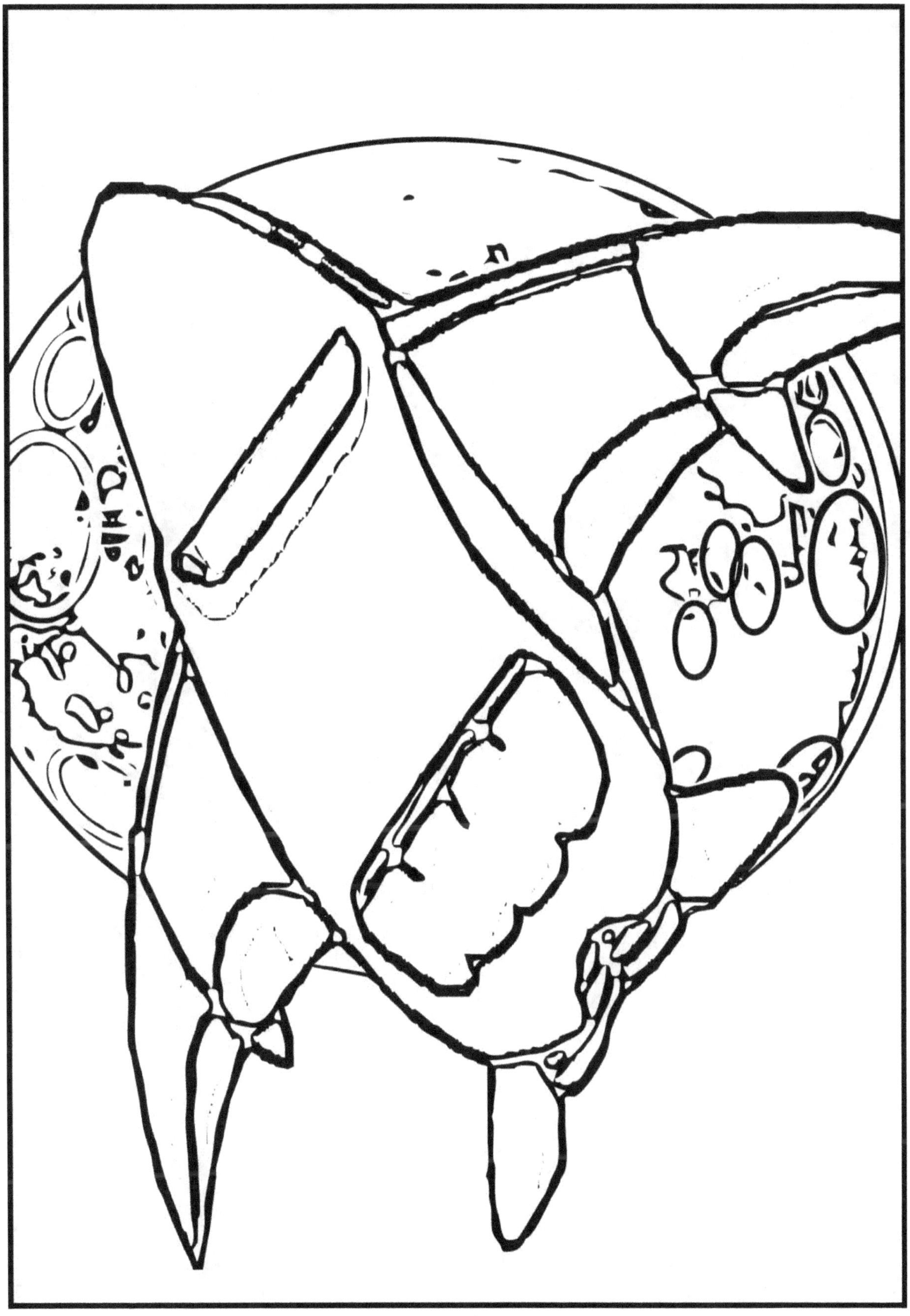

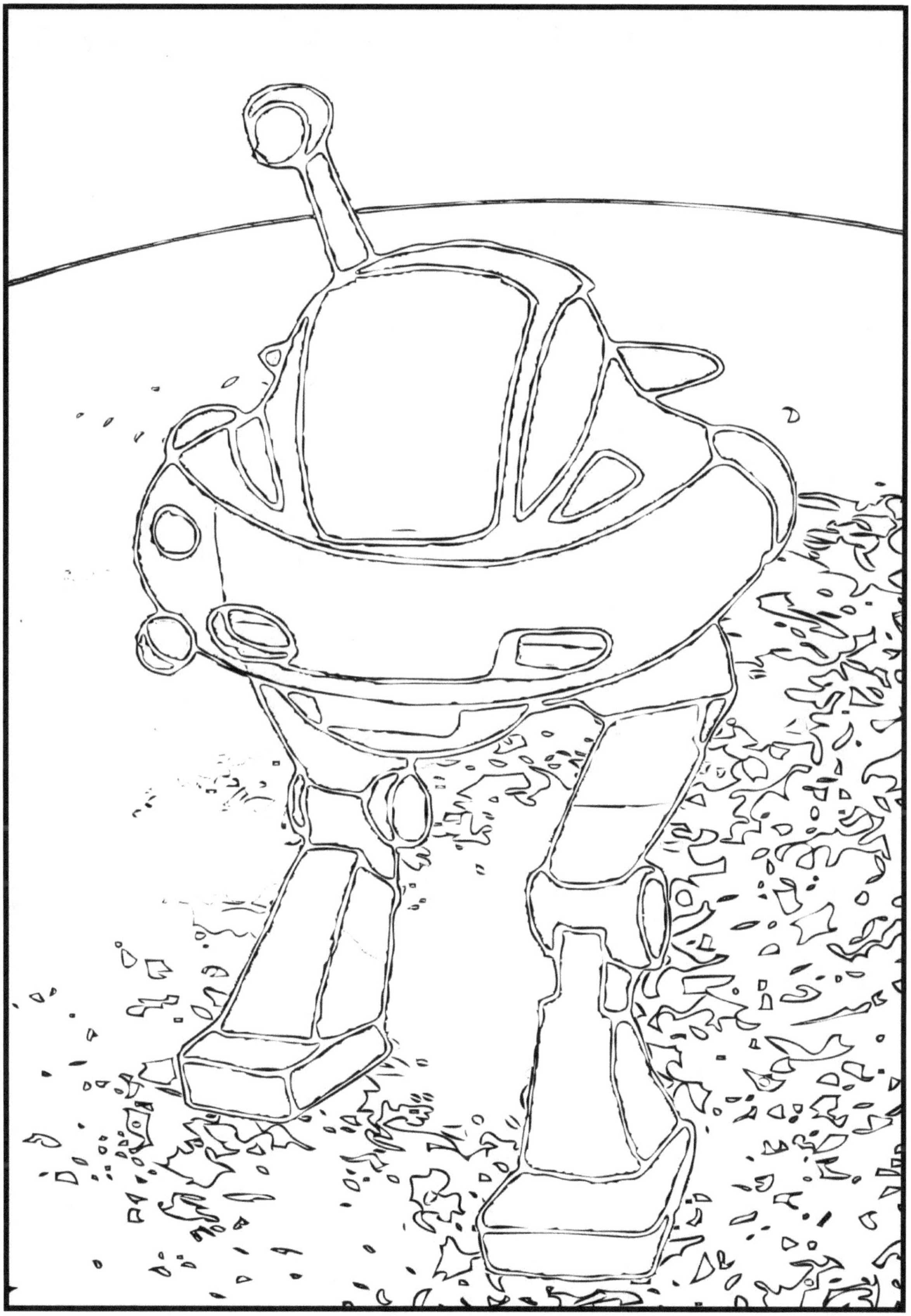

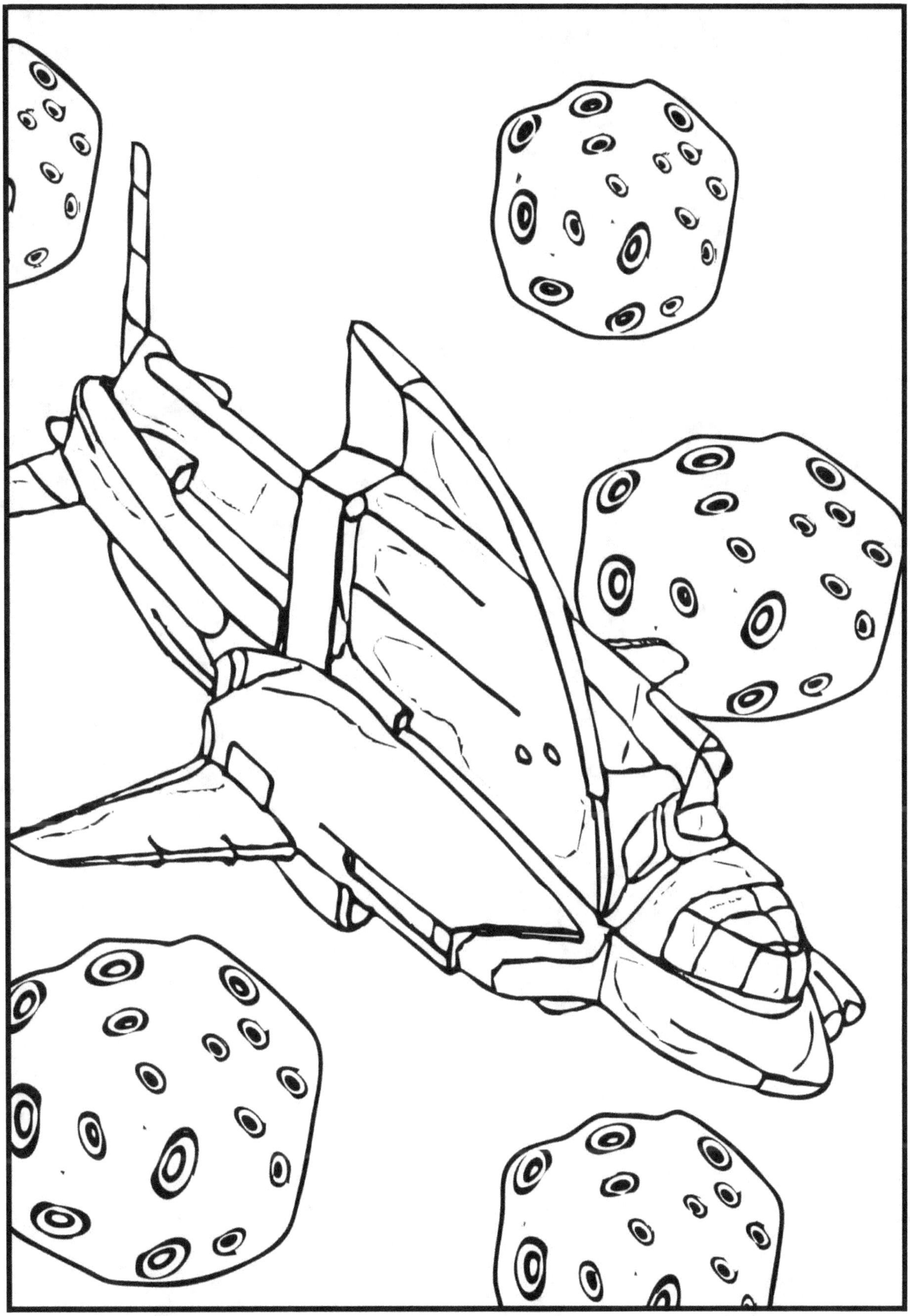

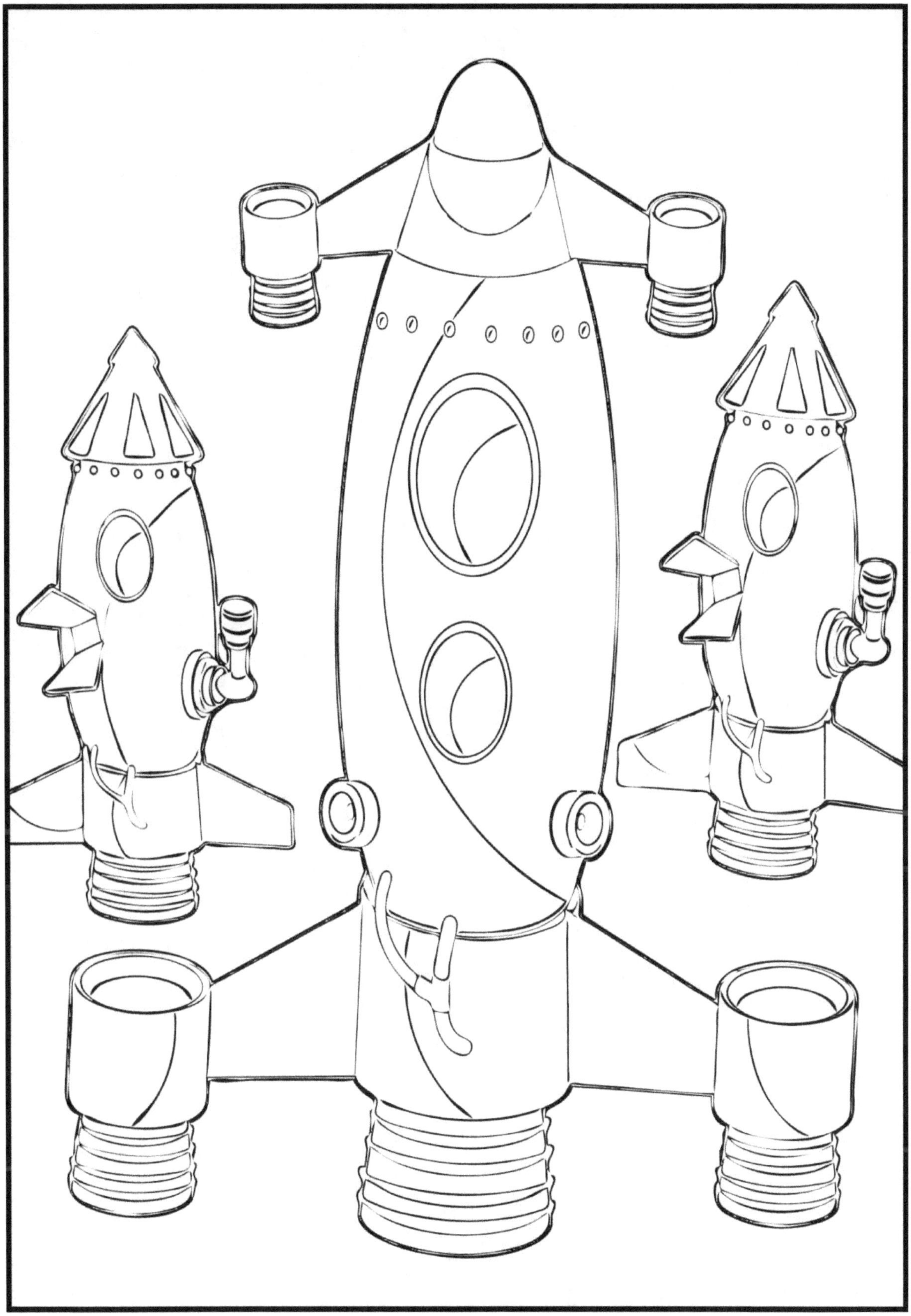

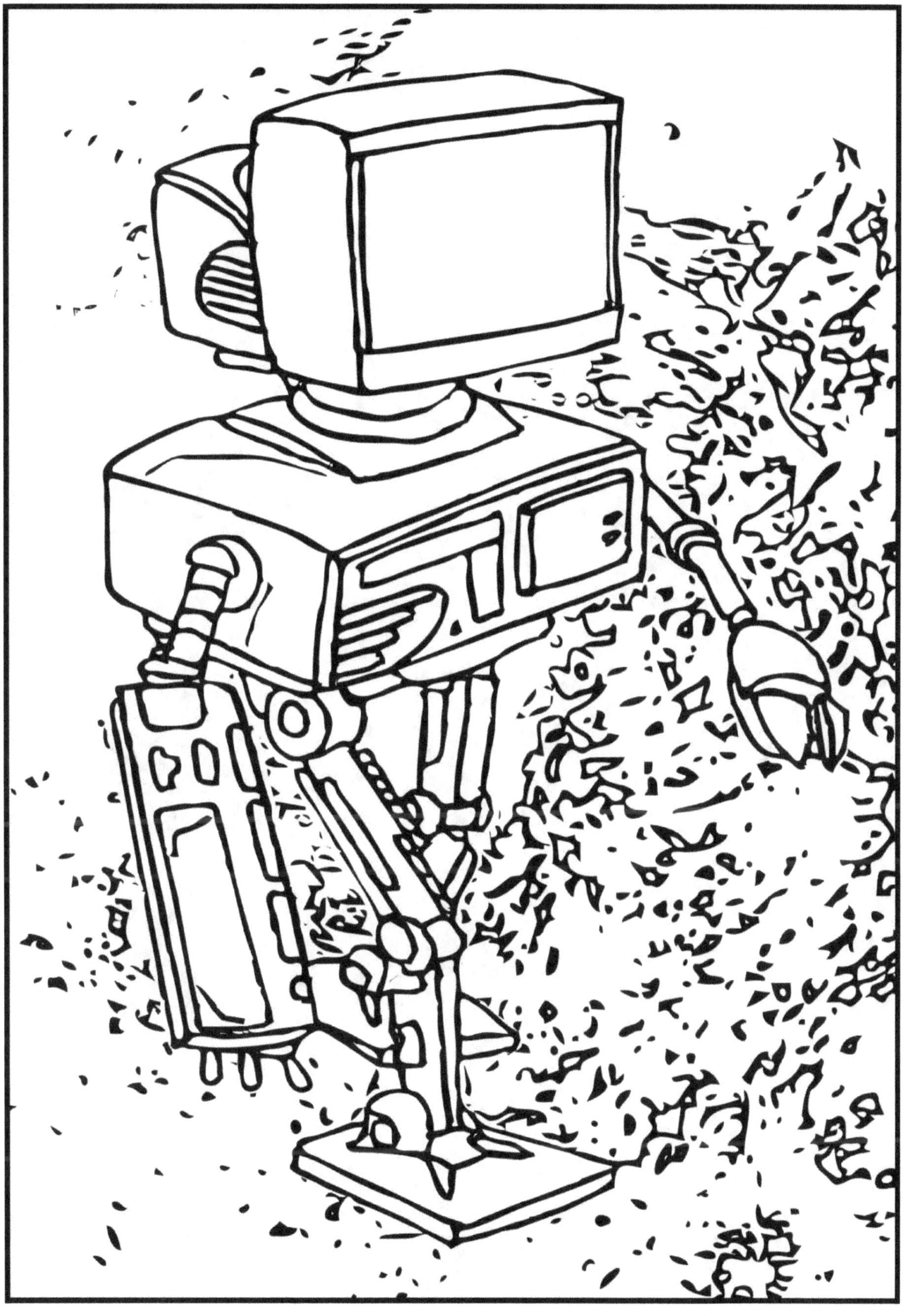

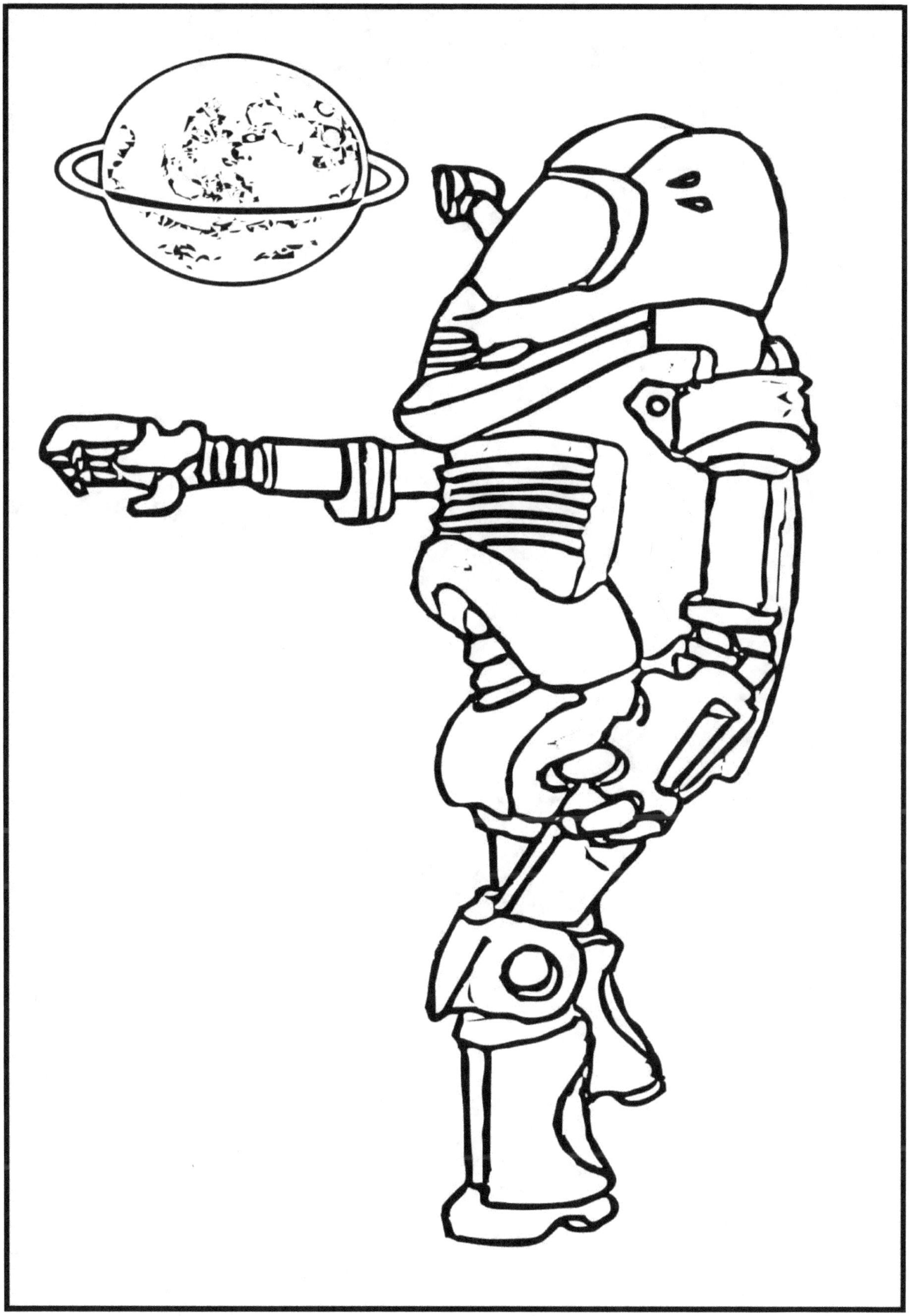

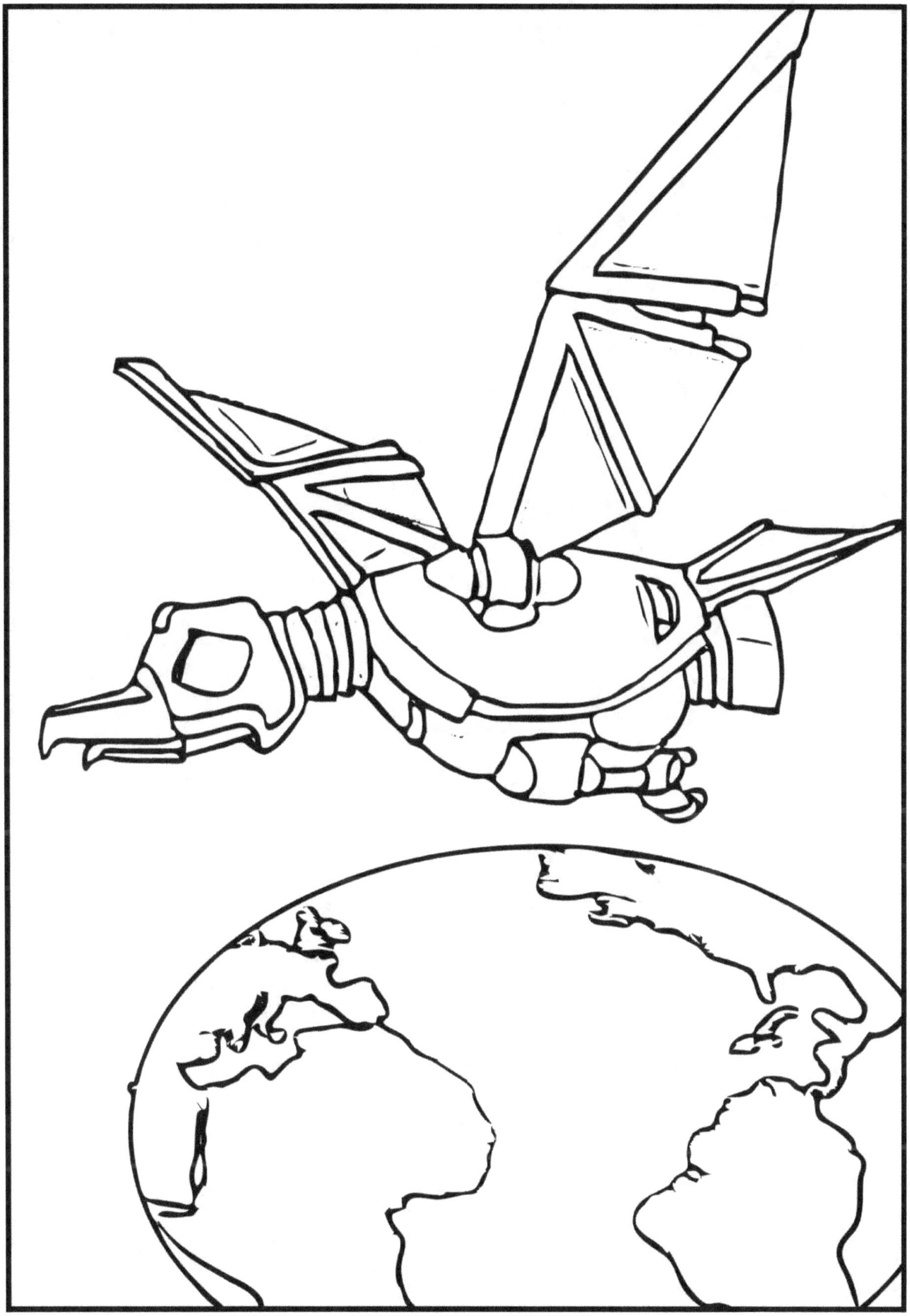

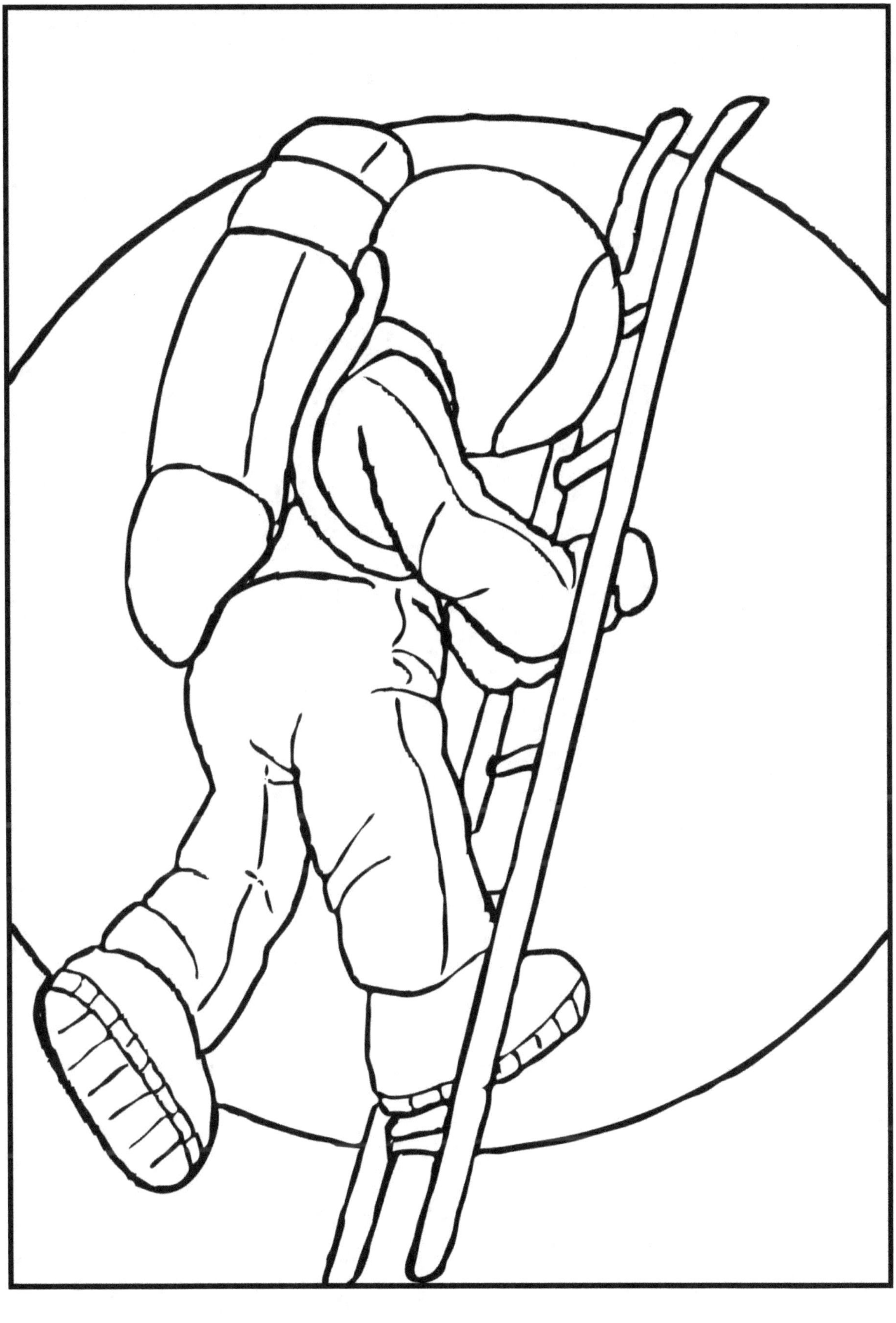

SCI FI
Coloring Book

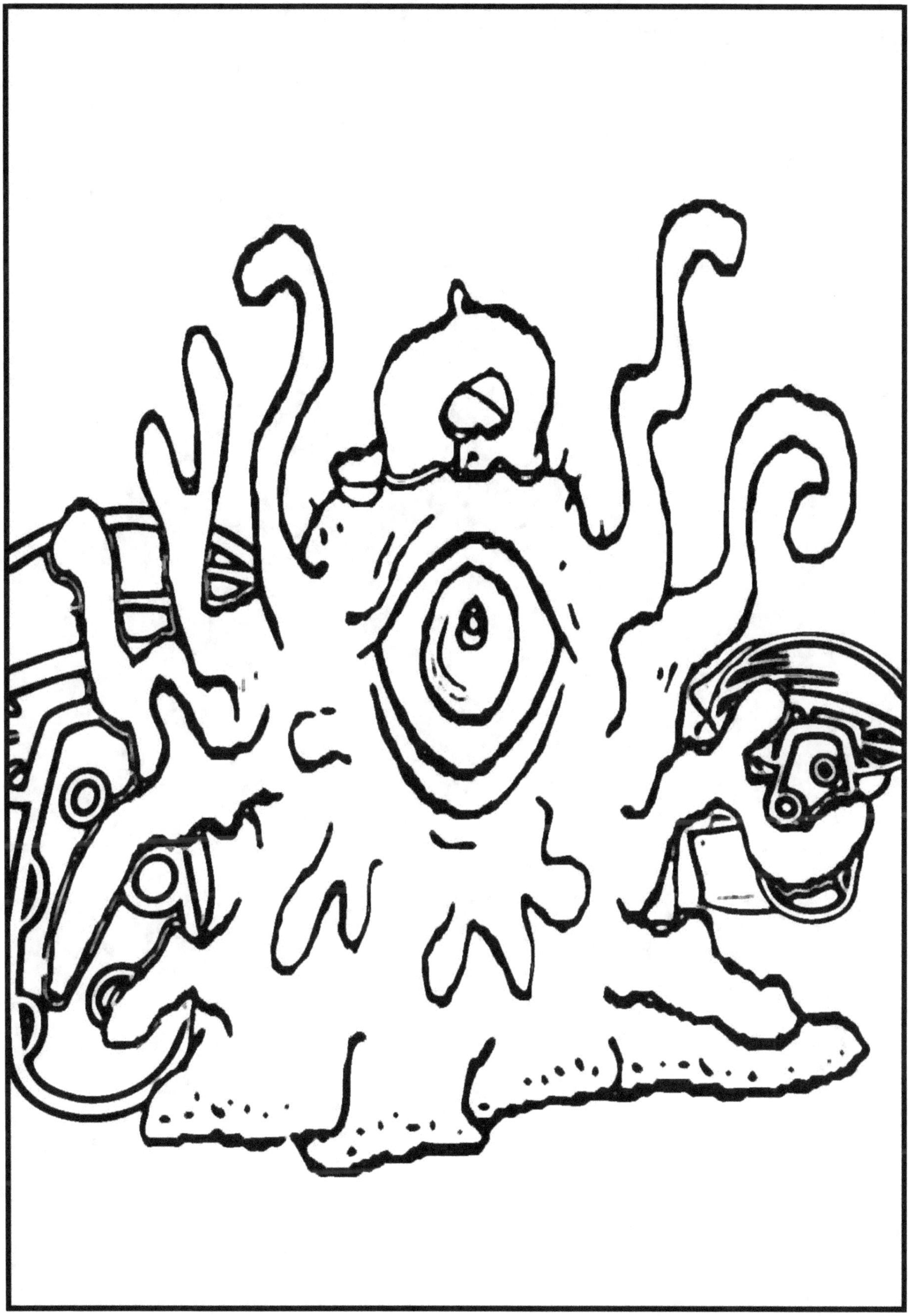

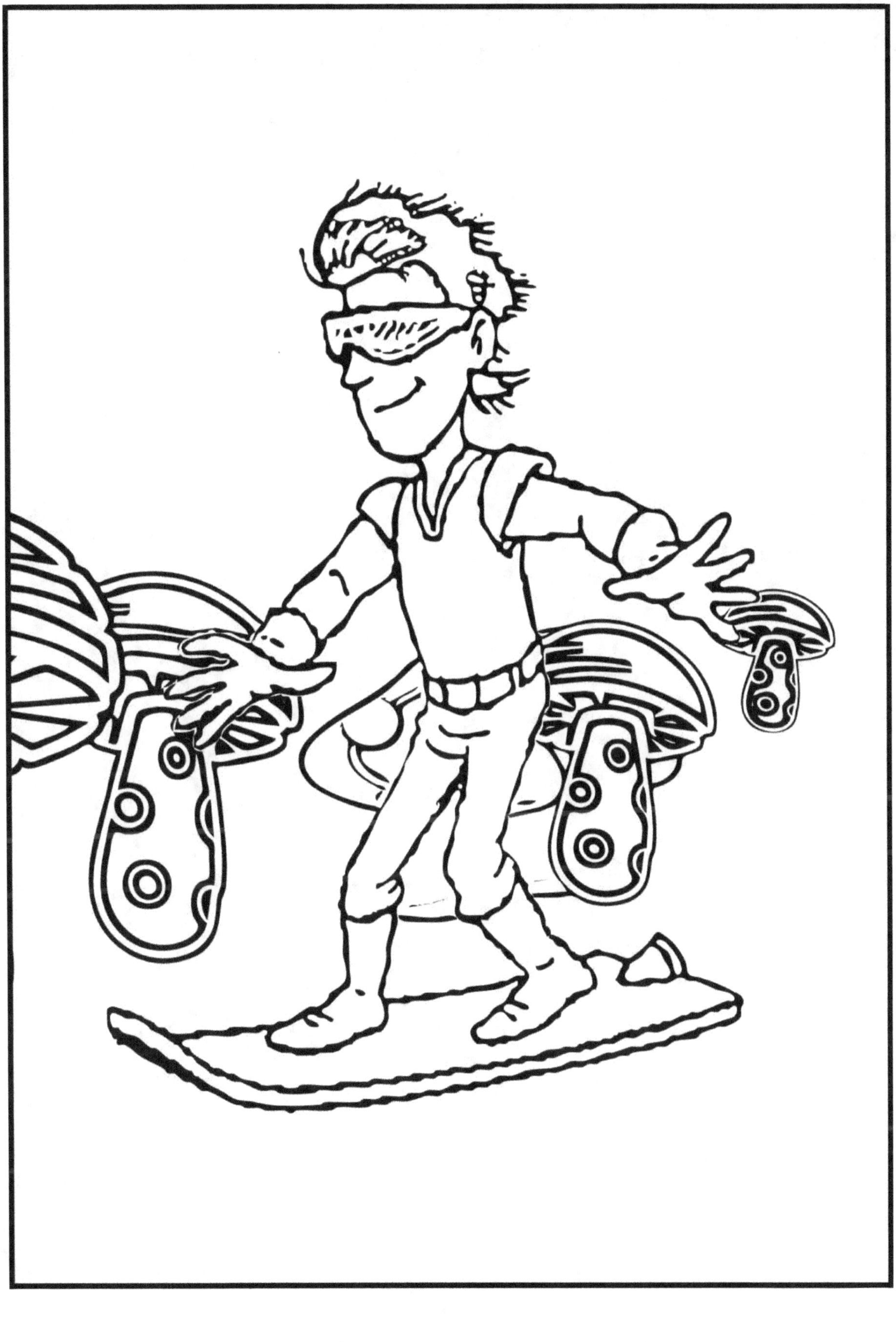

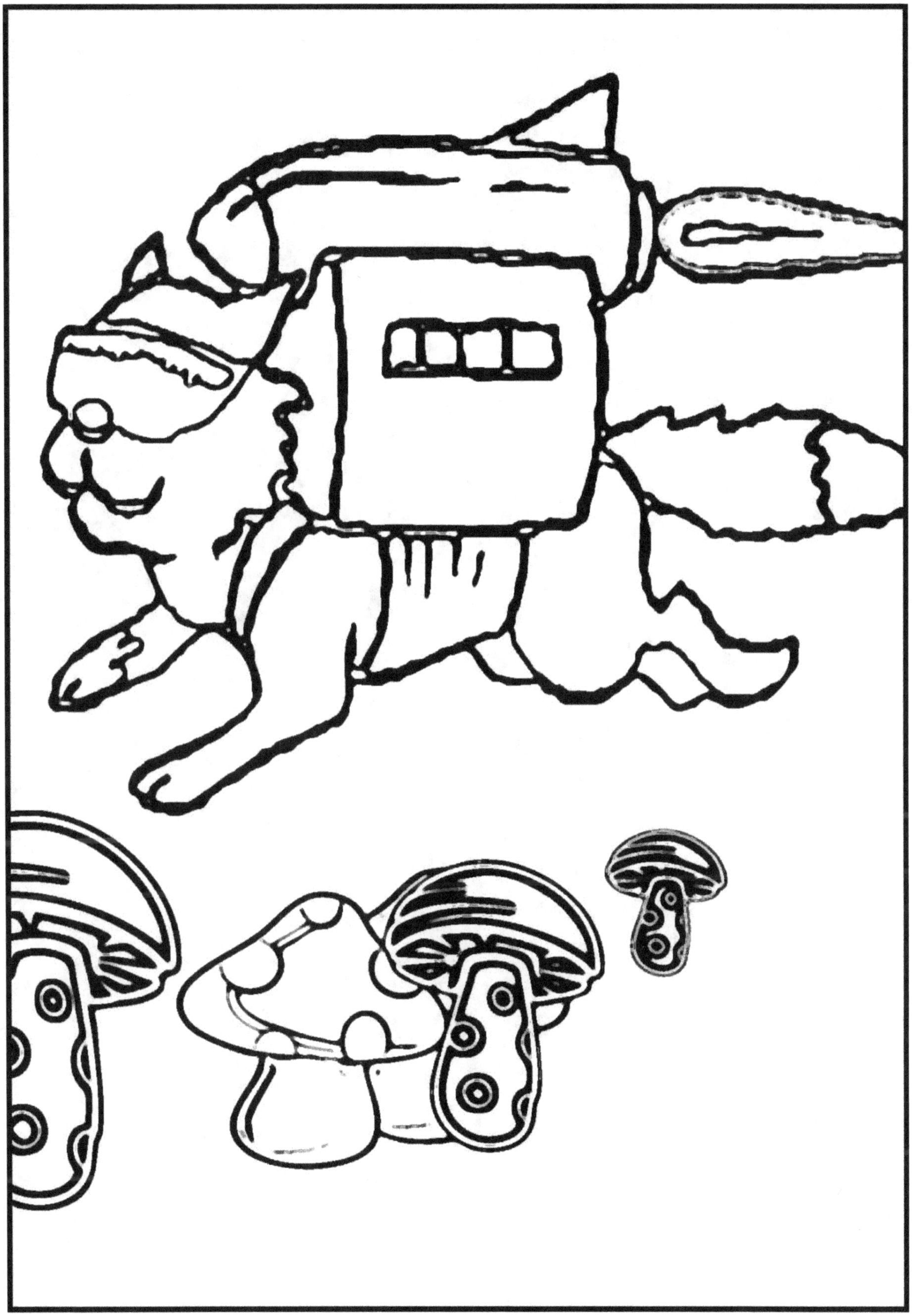

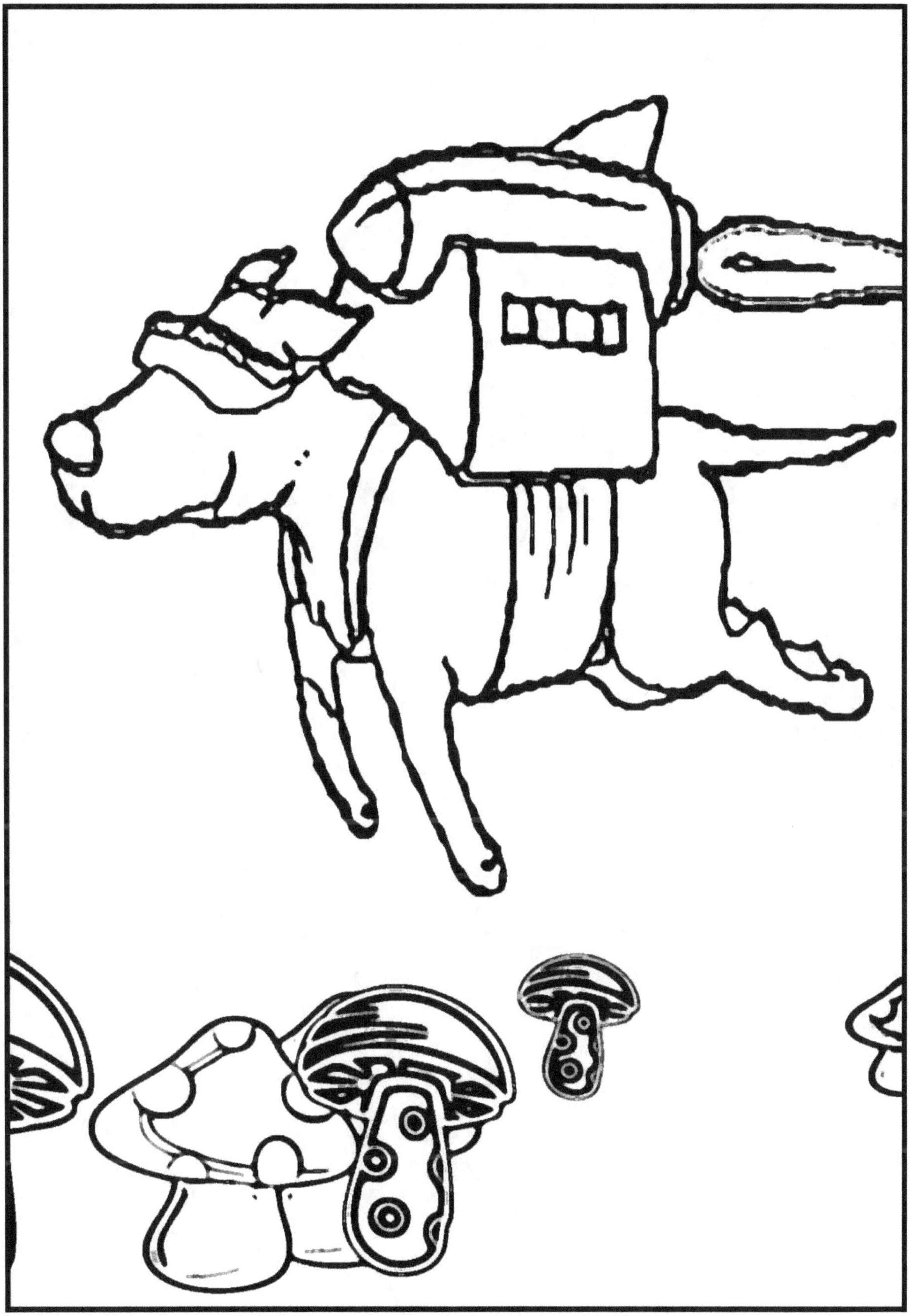

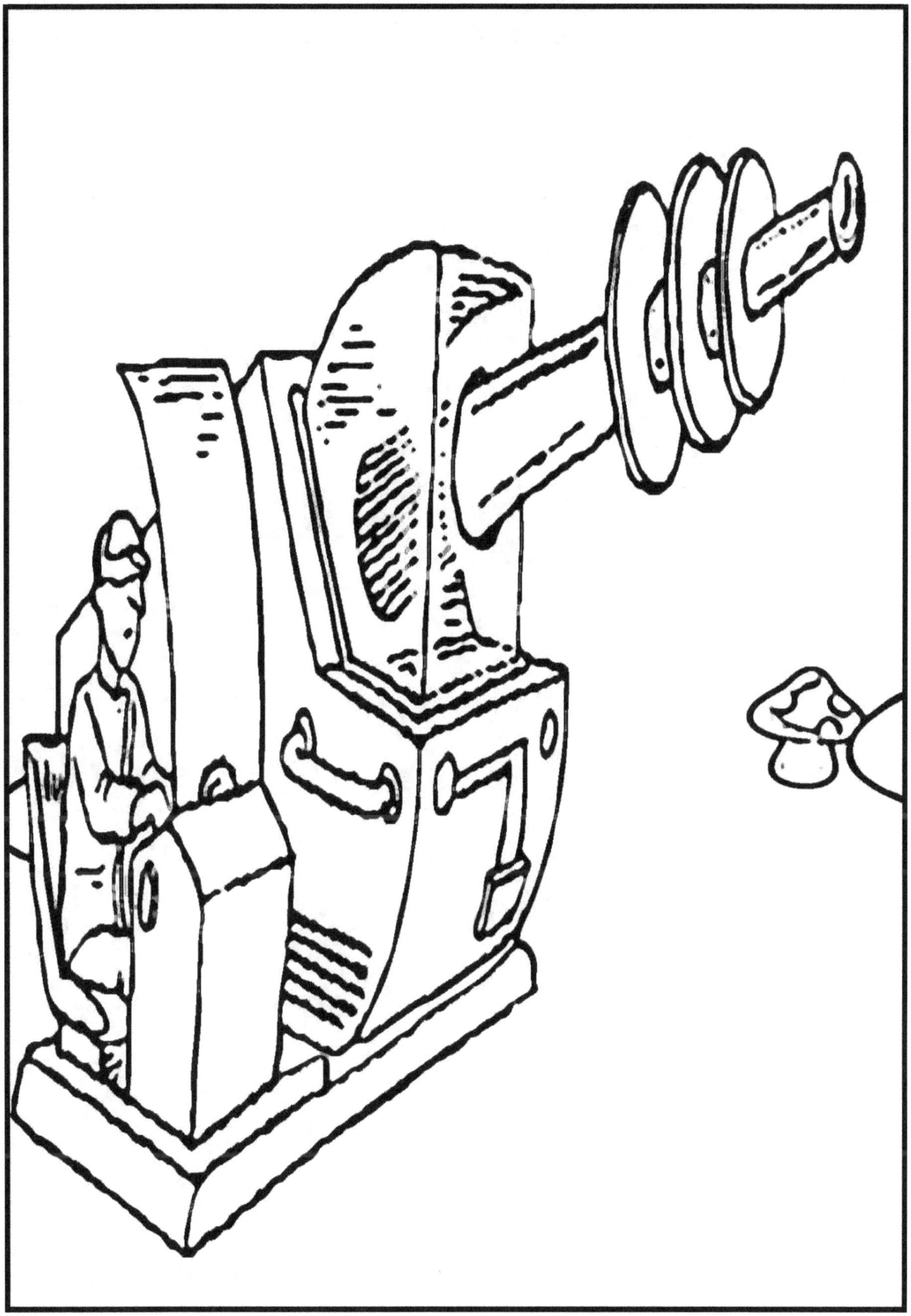

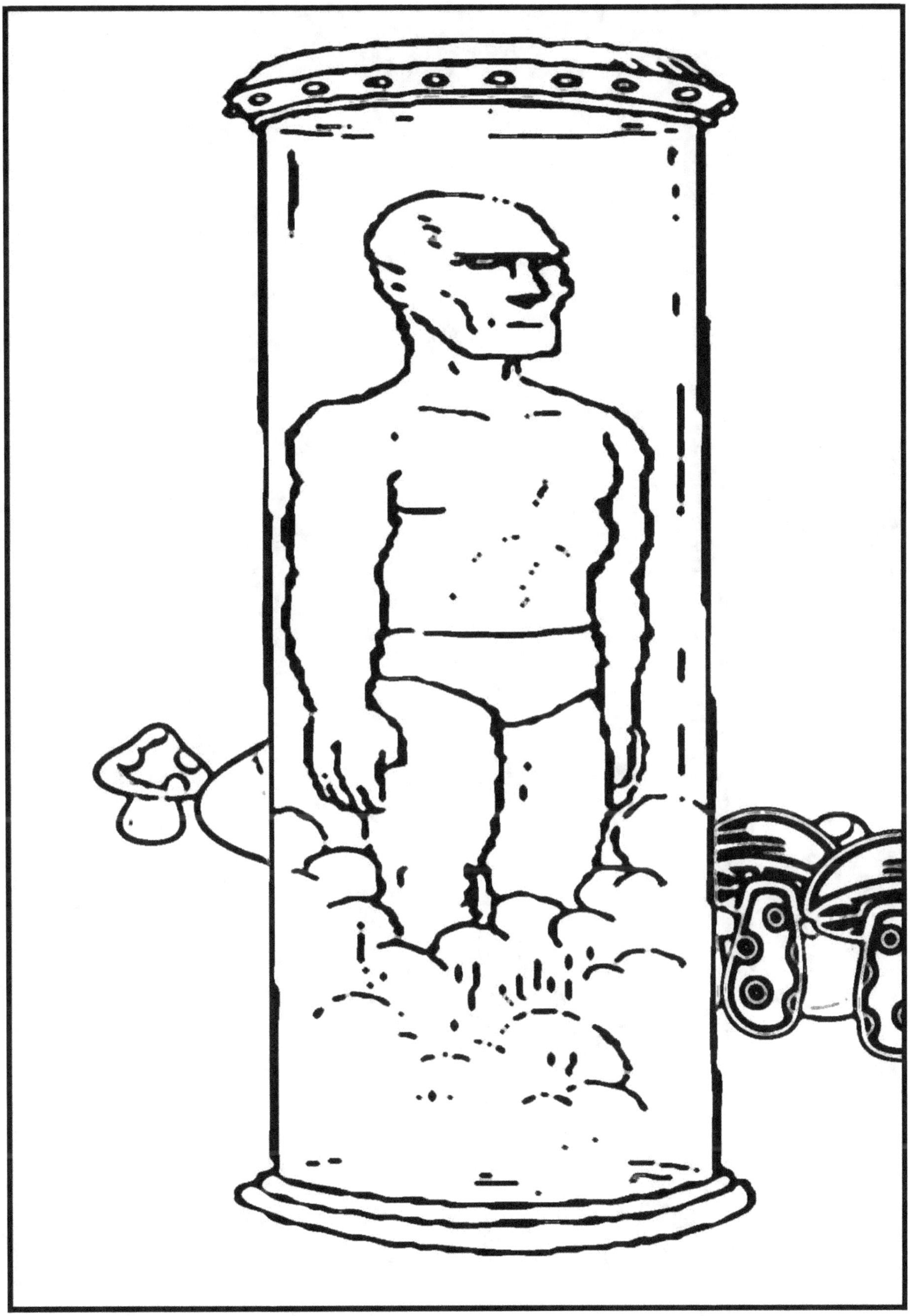

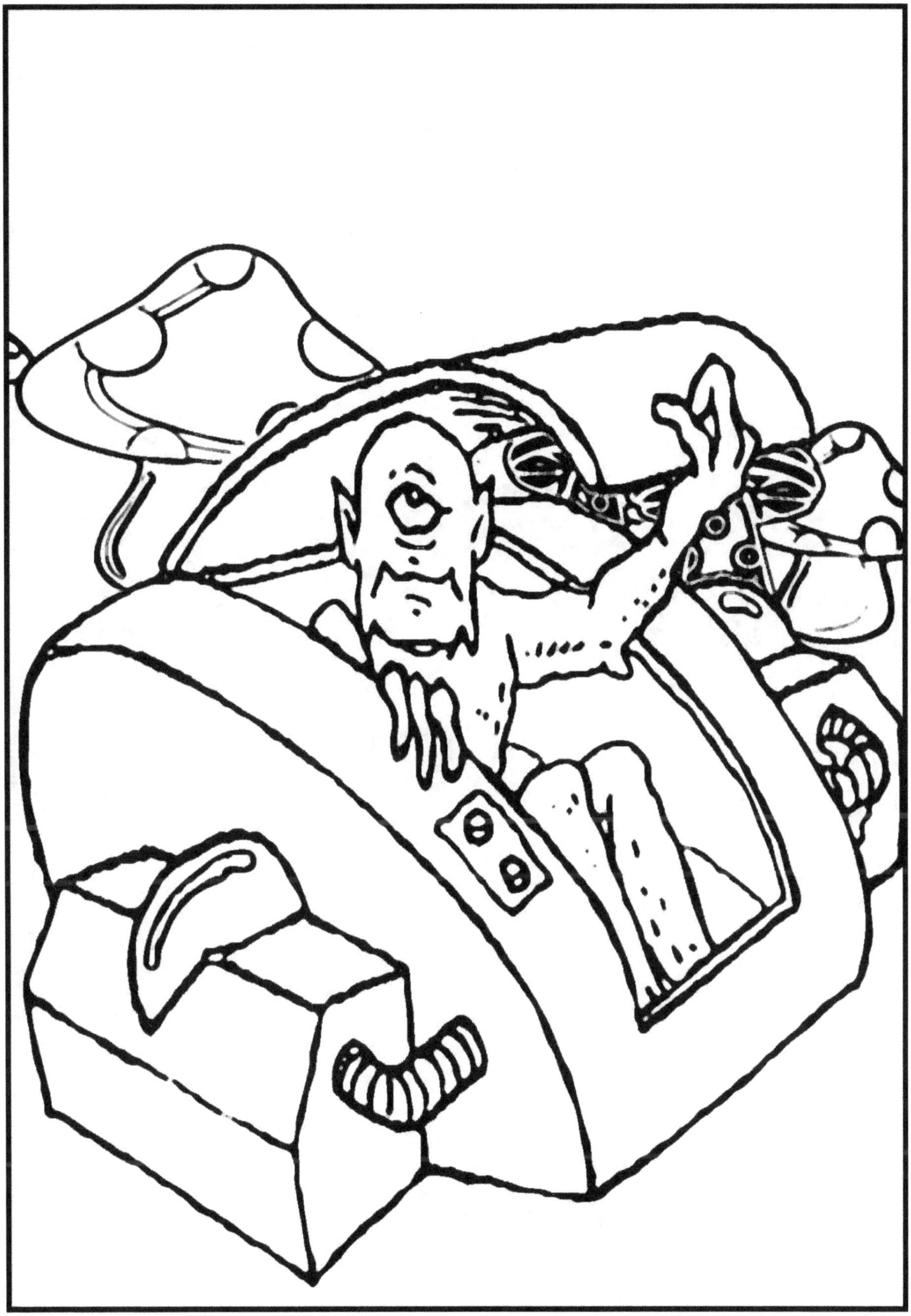

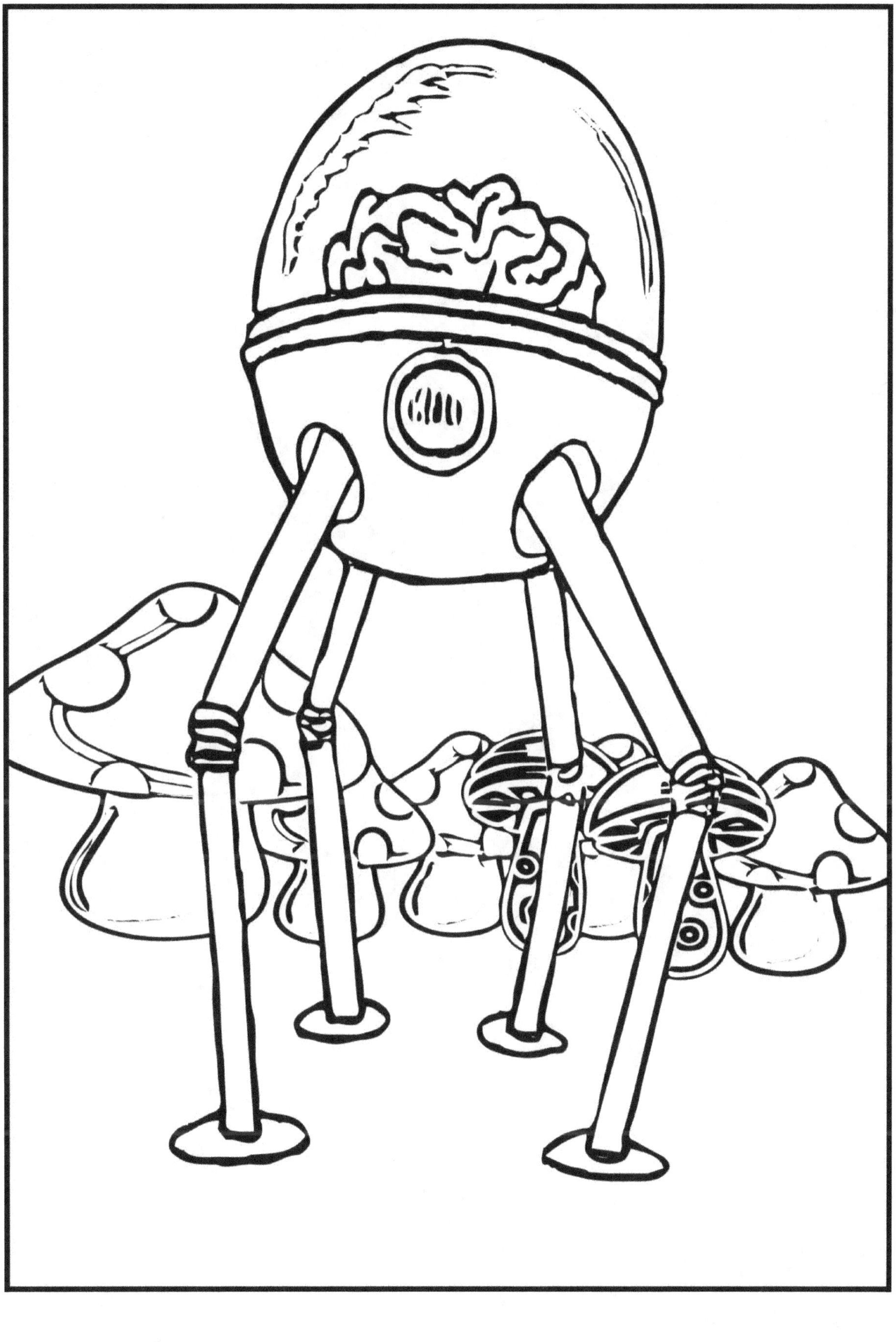

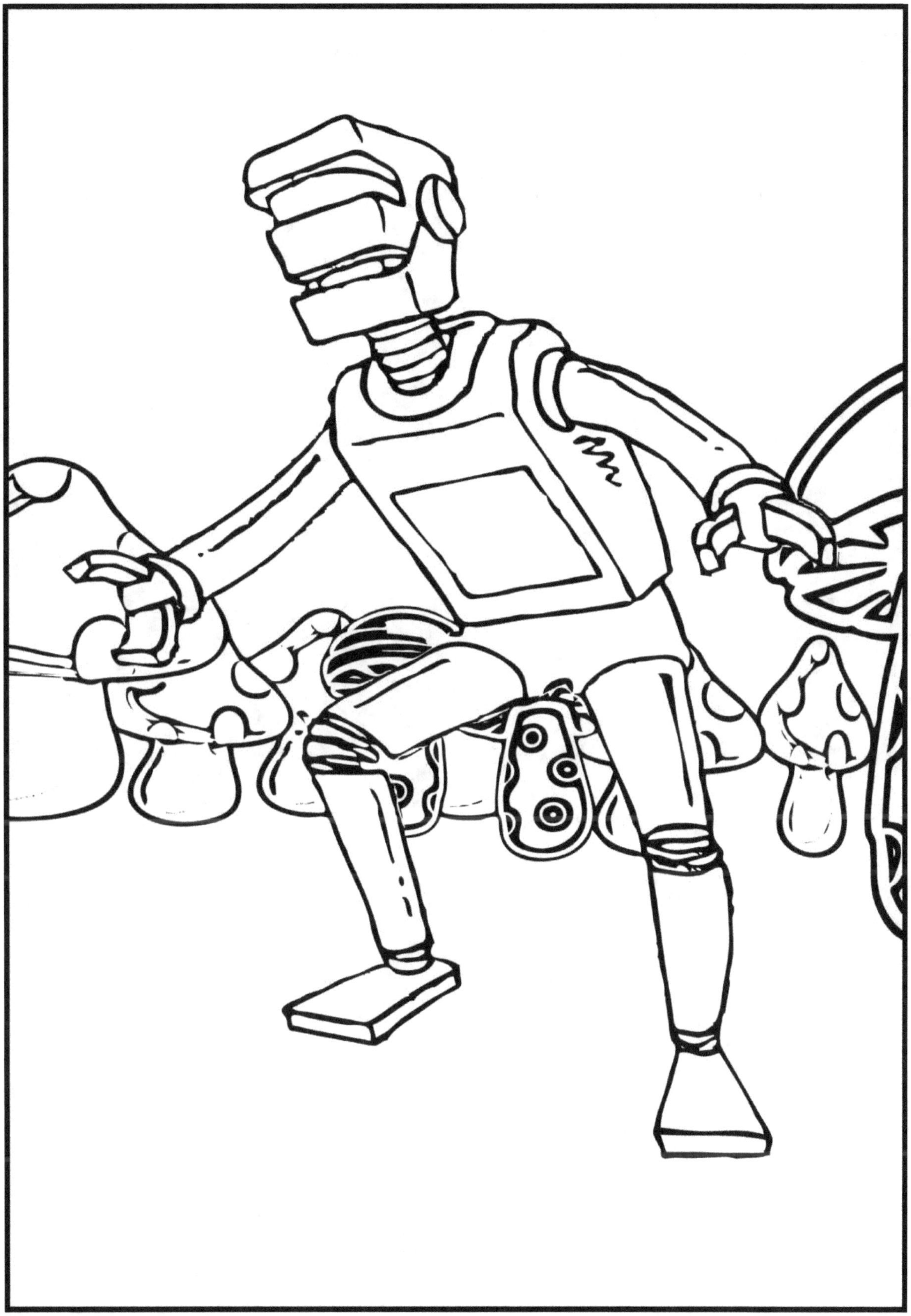

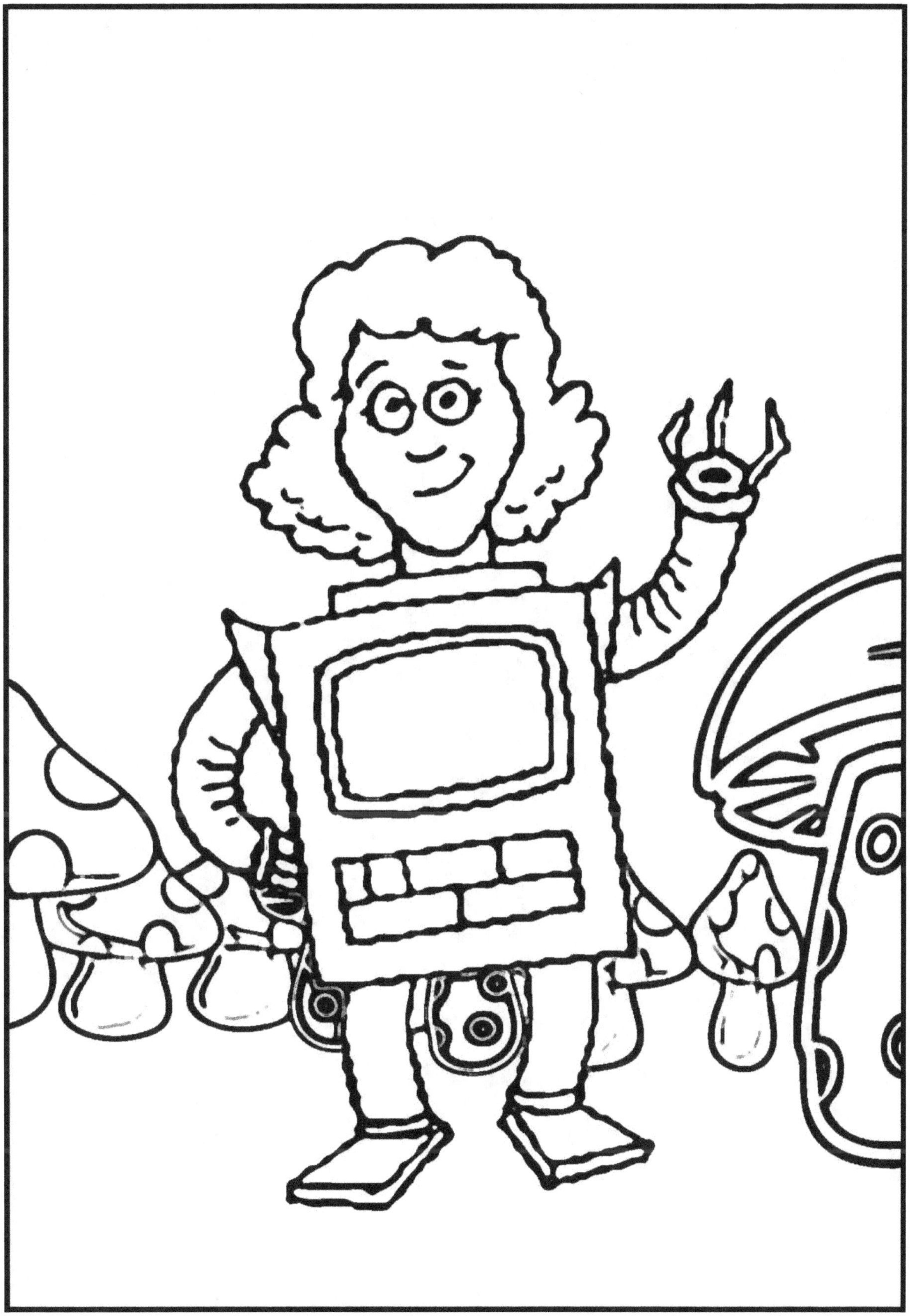

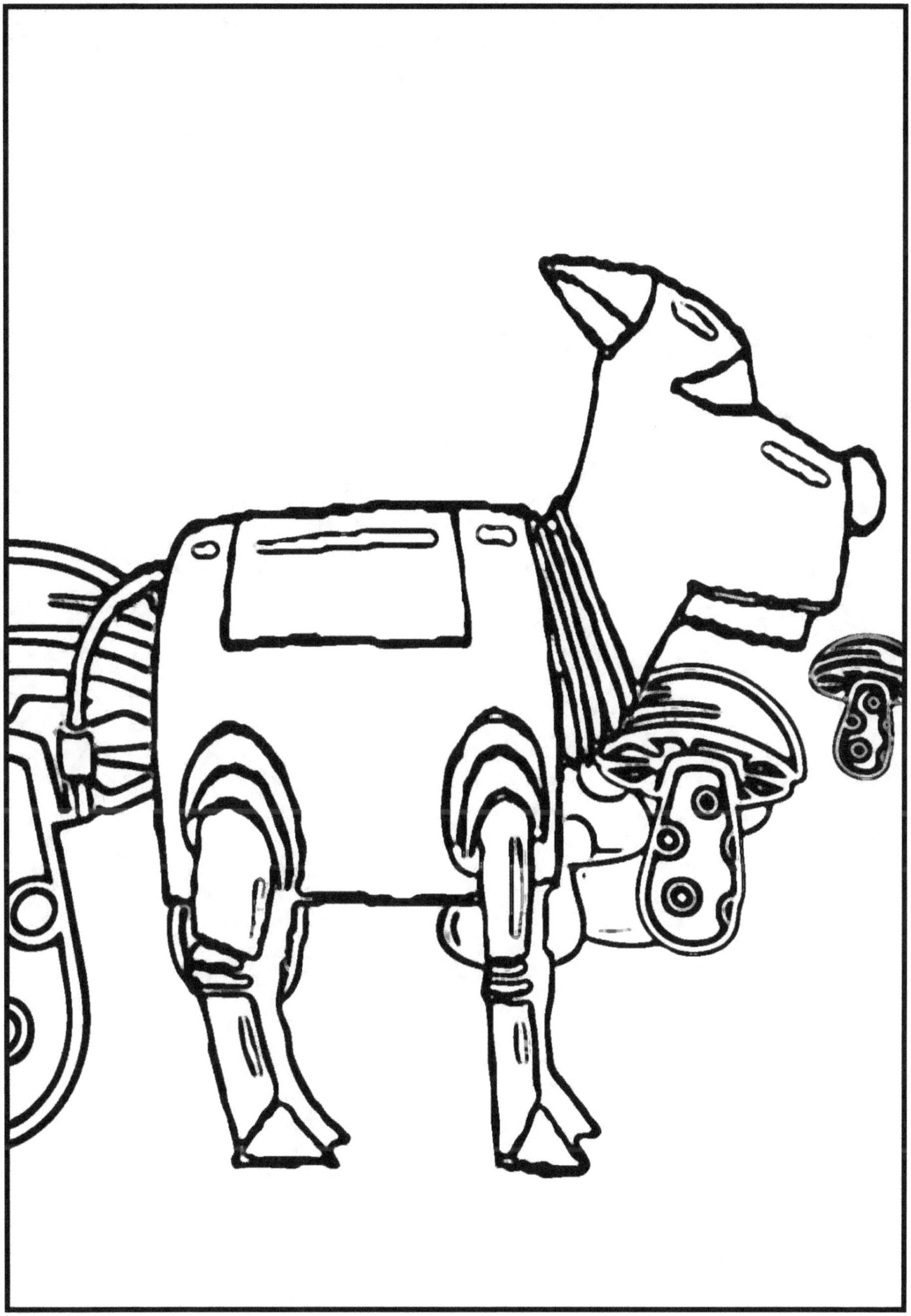

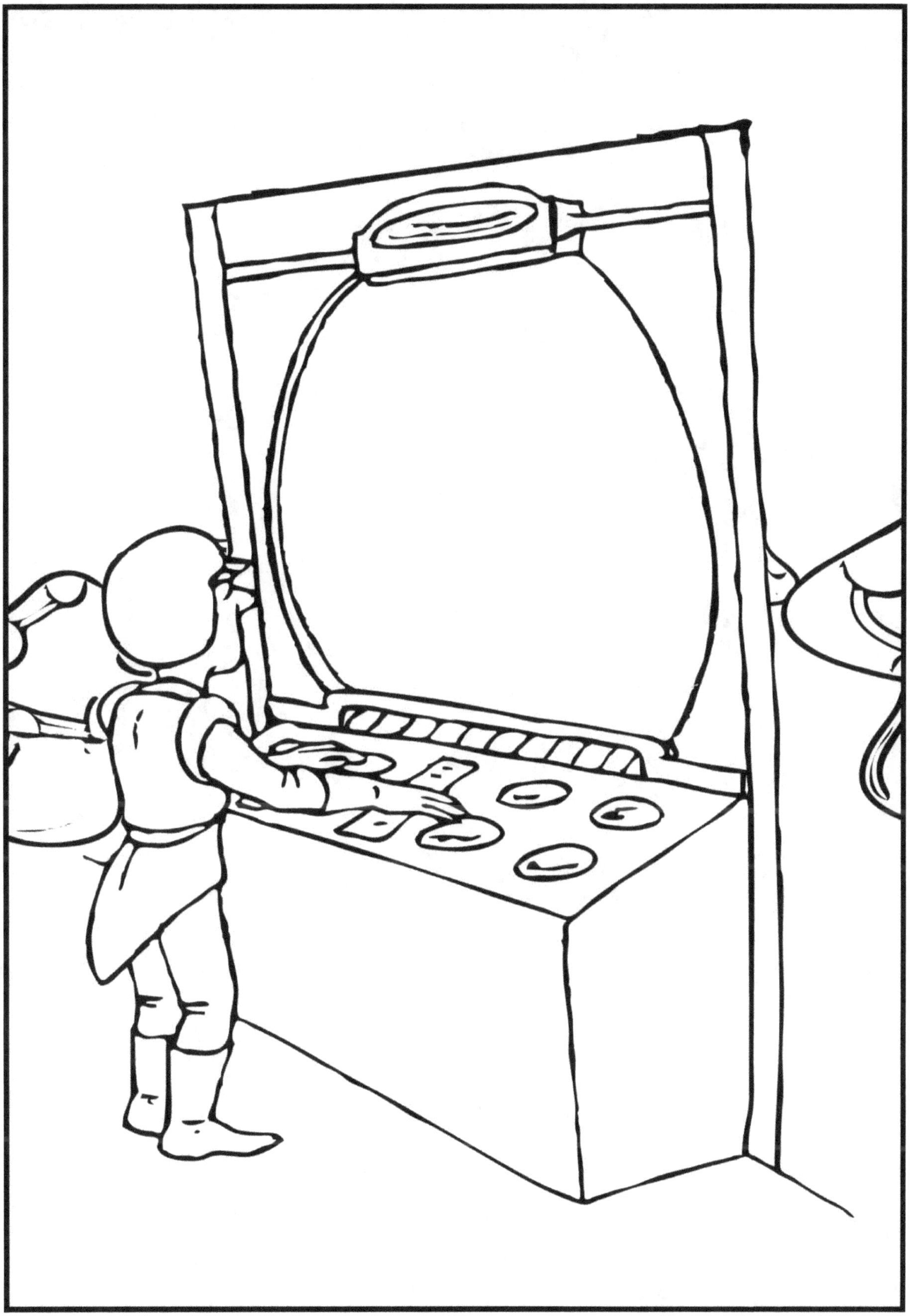

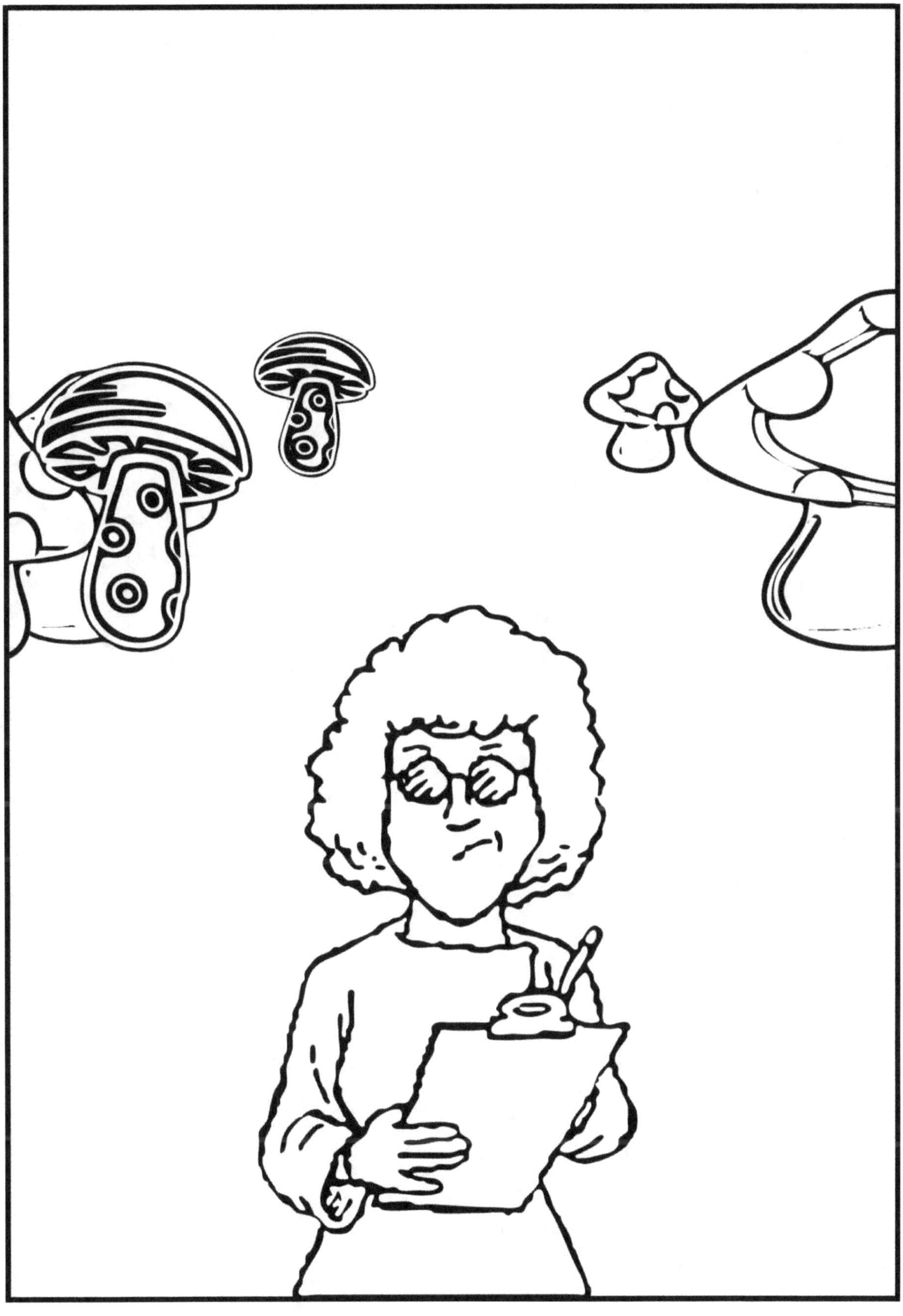

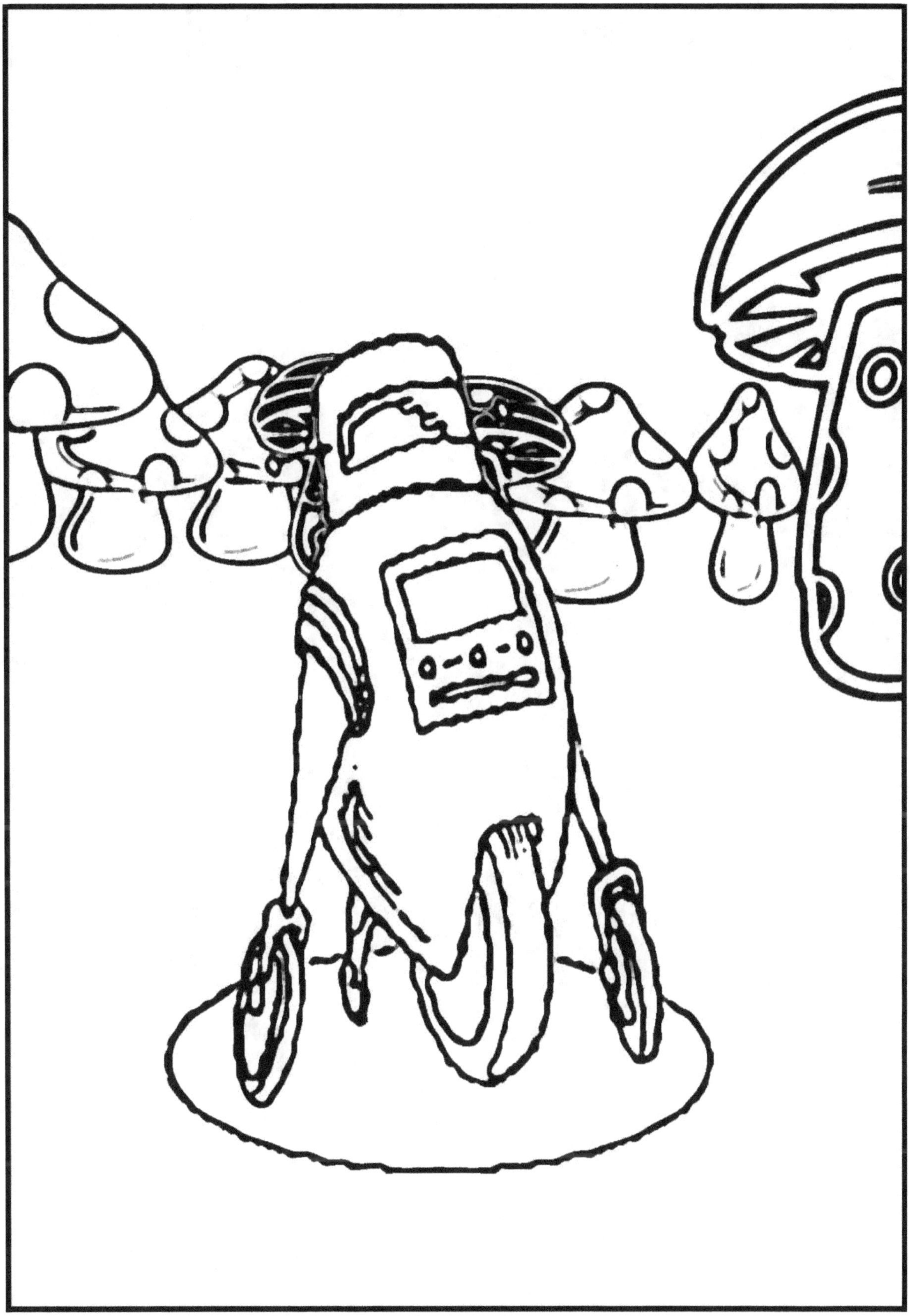

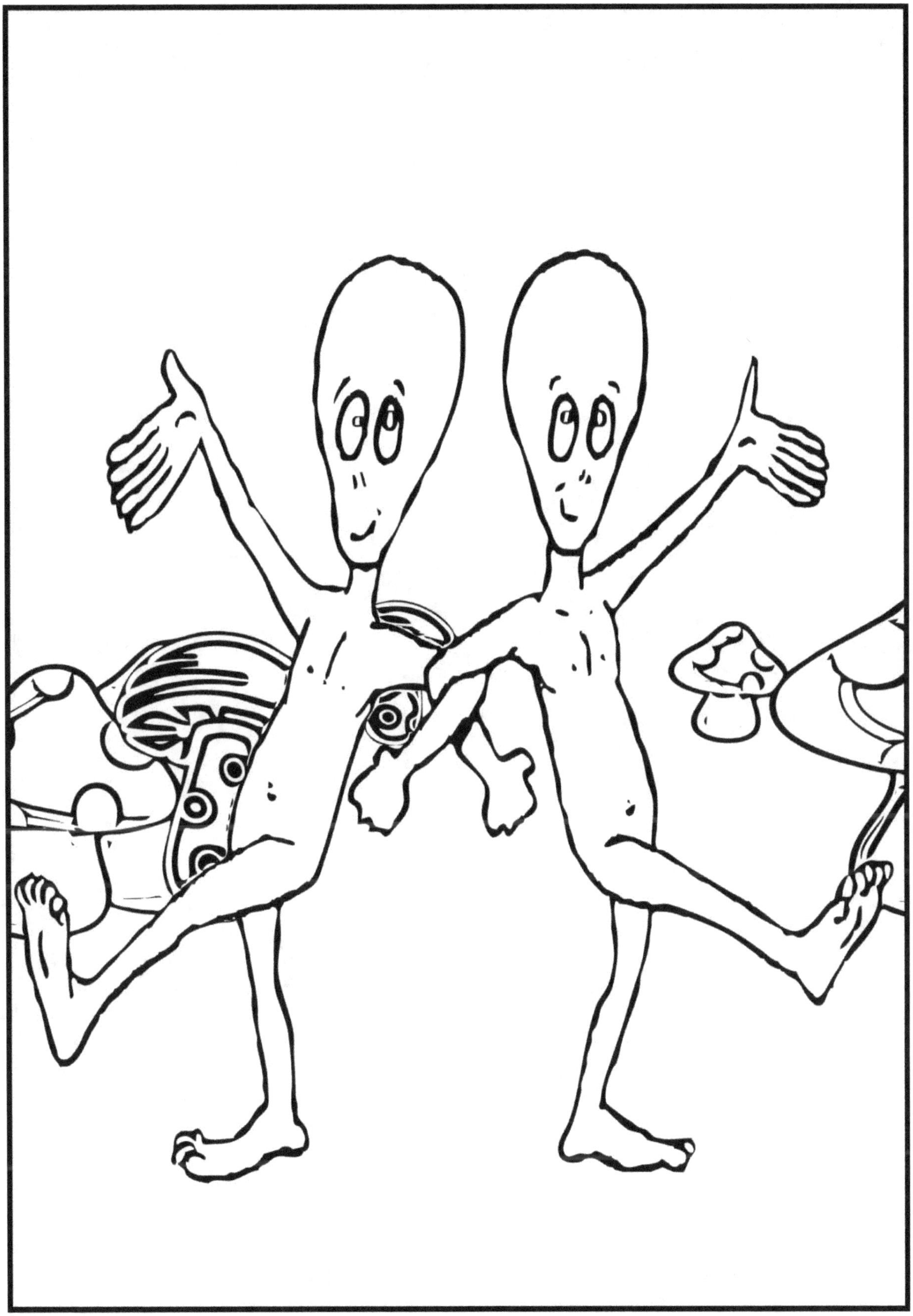

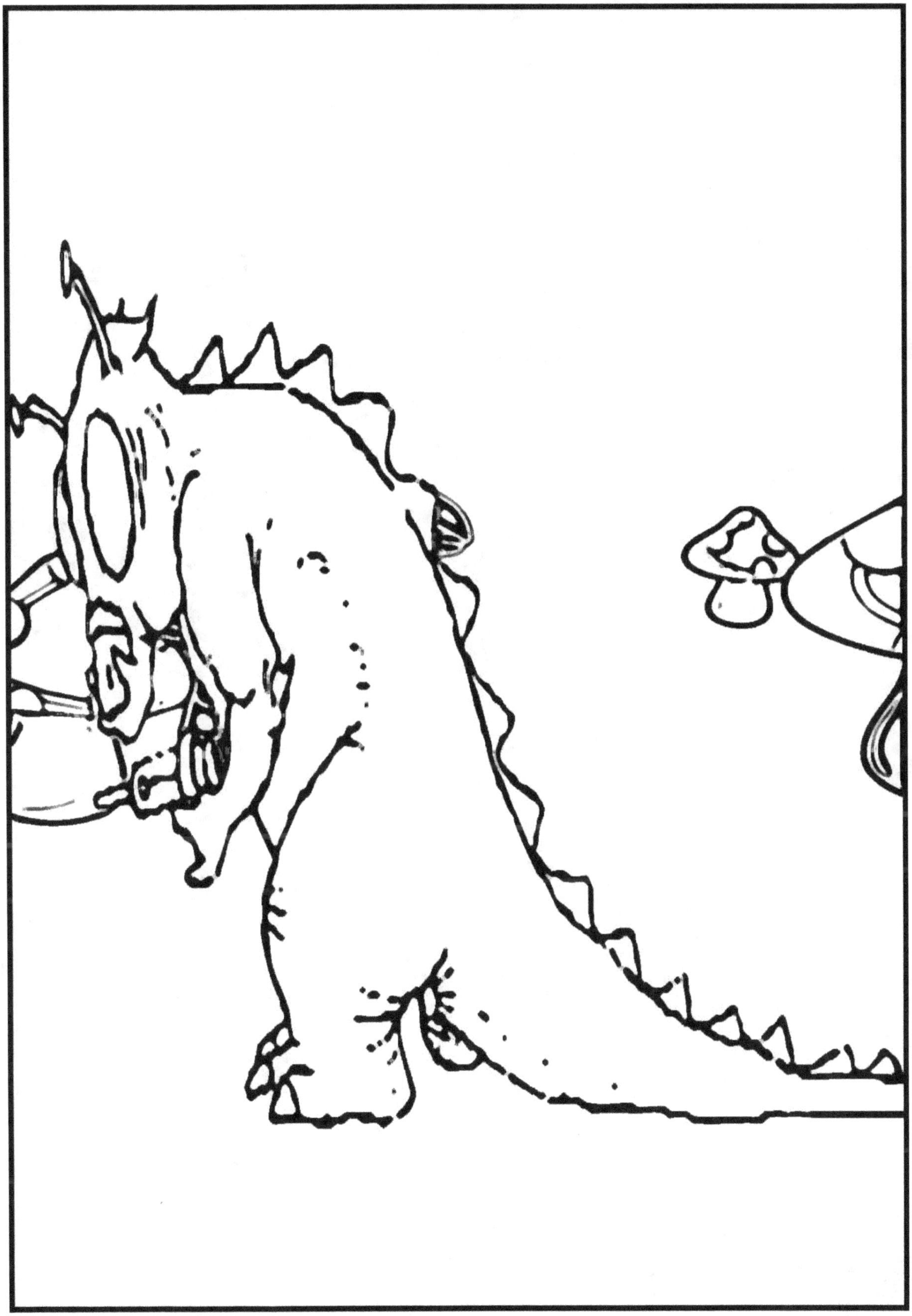

www.ingramcontent.com/pod-product-compliance
Lightning Source LLC
Chambersburg PA
CBHW081558170526
45166CB00009B/2745
* 9 7 8 1 5 1 9 6 6 8 6 0 8 *